Chosen

MICHELLE McCLAIN-WALTERS

CHARISMA
HOUSE

Most Charisma House Book Group products are available at special quantity discounts for bulk purchase for sales promotions, premiums, fund-raising, and educational needs. For details, call us at (407) 333-0600 or visit our website at www. charismahouse.com.

CHOSEN by Michelle McClain-Walters
Published by Charisma House
Charisma Media/Charisma House Book Group
600 Rinehart Road, Lake Mary, Florida 32746

Visit the author's website at www.michellemcclainwalters.com, michellemcclainbooks.com.

Library of Congress Cataloging-in-Publication Data

Names: McClain-Walters, Michelle, author.
Title: Chosen / by Michelle McClain-Walters.
Description: Lake Mary : Charisma House, 2019. | Includes bibliographical
  references. | Summary: "MANY ARE CALLED, BUT YOU ARE CHOSEN. This
  book
  will equip you with prophetic insight and divine strategies that will
  jump-start you on the path toward destiny. There is a distinction
  between the called and the chosen, the many and the few. Who are these
  people? How did they get exclusive access to the favor of God? They are
  confident and prosperous, generous and joyful. They live in the realm of
  miracles and the supernatural, as if the very breath of God is on every
  decision they make in life. One season after the next they are
  catapulted to new levels in life. All they do is win and trample over
  challenges, disappointments, and attacks from the enemy, while others
  still remain at the starting line, awaiting breakthrough. In her book
  Michelle McClain-Walters shows readers just what this distinction is and
  how they can live in the fullness of their identity as God's chosen
  ones. Built on the words of Christ in John 15:16-"You did not choose me,
  but I chose you and appointed you so that you might go and bear
  fruit-fruit that will last-and so that whatever you ask in my name the
  Father will give you"-and Matthew 22:14-"Many are called but few are
  chosen"-Chosen is a revelation of the spiritual force behind the life of
  the next-level believer. Choose now and declare, "I am chosen!" and
  watch as the mysteries of heaven are opened to you"-- Provided by
  publisher.
Identifiers: LCCN 2019025210 (print) | LCCN 2019025211 (ebook) | ISBN
  9781629996530 (trade paperback) | ISBN 9781629996547 (ebook)
Subjects: LCSH: Vocation--Christianity.
Classification: LCC BV4740 .M294 2019 (print) | LCC BV4740 (ebook) | DDC
  248.4--dc23
LC record available at https://lccn.loc.gov/2019025210
LC ebook record available at https://lccn.loc.gov/2019025211

This publication is translated in Spanish under the title *Escogidos*, copyright ©
2020 by Michelle McClain-Walters, published by Casa Creación, a Charisma Media
company. All rights reserved.

19 20 21 22 23—987654321
Printed in the United States of America

CONTENTS

FOREWORD

GOD HAS ALWAYS chosen men and women to do great things to fulfill His plans and purposes. The call and responsibility of being chosen have always been exciting and challenging. God gives special mandates, commissions, and assignments with the necessary talents, abilities, gifts, and anointing to fulfill these special plans and purposes.

In this book Michelle McClain-Walters explains the dynamics of being chosen. Her insight comes from personal experience and the Word of God. Michelle has a strong desire to see believers walk in their special callings. She is a prophetic minister, and prophets by nature are concerned about the plans and purposes of God and the role of men and women in those plans.

God chooses us by His grace. We cannot boast or take pride in being chosen. Being chosen will humble you, and it will challenge you. The chosen are often chosen in the "furnace of affliction" (Isa. 48:10, KJV). The chosen live and walk by God's grace and power. The enemy hates the chosen because they release great blessings to people.

God uses His chosen ones to bring miracles, salvation, healing, deliverance, restoration, breakthrough, change, and upgrade.

This book will encourage you in your calling and assignment. Every believer is chosen to do something. You are responsible for your gifts and calling. You cannot neglect them. You must stir up your gifts and move out in faith. Your obedience is necessary to see the glory of God manifest on your behalf. You will see many miracles manifest through being the vessel God had chosen you to be. Someone's life depends on your obedience.

The responsibility of the chosen is great. Unto whom much is given much is required (Luke 12:48). There are many truths to be learned from the lives of those who were chosen before us. In this book Michelle examines the lives of chosen ones. Their lives are meant to encourage us to reach our generation and impact generations to come.

I pray that you will receive the necessary courage, boldness, inspiration, and revelation to fulfill the call upon your life. This book will motivate you to obey God and do what He has called you to do. You are not alone. God is on your side. Everything you need to complete your assignment has been provided for you. May the truths shared in this book mobilize you to do mighty works and great exploits.

—JOHN ECKHARDT
OVERSEER, CRUSADERS MINISTRIES

Introduction

LIFESTYLE OF THE CALLED AND CHOSEN

For many are called, but few are chosen.
—MATTHEW 22:14

I T HAS BEEN prophesied for centuries, but the day has now come for the righteous generation to arise. This is the day when God is raising up a righteous people who feel the eternal weight of glory bearing upon their spirits, and they will produce a wave of God's glory and power in the earth that manifests like an explosion, shaking every nation, kindred, tongue, and people.

This is who the chosen are. This is how they live. Their lives are propelled like a missile by a spiritual force that comes straight from the throne room of God. Because of their chosen status, God sets the coordinates for their lives and they are launched forward, and nothing is able to stop them. They do not veer to the right or to the left. The chosen are those who have responded to the call of God to represent His kingdom on earth. God is not a respecter of persons; He is a respecter of faith. The chosen ones are those who have determined to seek the kingdom of God and His righteousness. They have made the decision to represent Jesus Christ in the earth.

The lifestyle of a chosen one is a whole other level of living with the power of heaven fully activated in the earth realm, and it is available only to those who will maintain the standard of righteousness God requires. This is the eternal and uncompromising weight of glory that God is placing upon the shoulders of a select group of people who will bear His fruit. He tells us so in John 15:16 (AMP):

> You have not chosen Me, but I have chosen you and I
> have appointed and placed and purposefully planted
> you, so that you would go and bear fruit and keep
> on bearing, and that your fruit will remain and be
> lasting, so that whatever you ask of the Father in
> My name [as My representative] He may give to you.

Chosen. Appointed. Placed. Purposefully planted, as His representatives, to bear fruit and keep bearing fruit that will remain. And *then* whatever they ask in His name is theirs. Some people try to skip right to that last part. But to have whatever we ask, we must first be chosen. And God has a standard and requirements in place for those who would dare cross over into the chosen realm. Is the chosen realm your realm?

If He has called many but chosen a few, how do you know if you are called or chosen? How does the chosen lifestyle and experience with God differ from the average believer's? Is everyone chosen? If not, then who are the chosen? Who are those whom God chooses? Let's see what makes up the lifestyle and identity of a chosen one; then you make the call—are you chosen?

THE CHOSEN WALK IN THE EXCELLENCE OF GOD'S POWER

But we have this treasure in earthen vessels, that the excellence of the power may be of God and not of us.
—2 CORINTHIANS 4:7

Living life as a chosen one is not about us. It is about the power of God. If we have been chosen, His hand is upon us and we are going to carry *His* glory to the ends of the earth. When we interact with the broken, rejected, abandoned, and even the angry, perverse, and rebellious, we will confront the strongholds working in them and speak the truth to them in love. They will hear the truth and be set free.

So many people want to compromise the truth in order to stay out of the spotlight and avoid being labeled a hater. But even when it comes to the sway of our culture toward things that God calls an abomination, the chosen walk in a level of glory that comes with a confrontational anointing. The chosen do not fear man; they fear God. Their first concern is to simply say and do what God tells them to say and do. Their obedience will release a glory that draws attention. When the TV cameras come, all each one will say is, "It's of God and not of me. This is not what I say. It's what God says."

The chosen are a prophetic people. No matter how many people are perverting the truth of God's Word, they will preach and live the truth and nothing but the truth. This is why they can claim God's promise that "I'll make your name great, and the nations shall come up to you." (See Genesis 12:2.) This is why they are able to walk unapologetically in the favor of God. They have earned God's trust on things that are important to Him, and He releases power and promotion over their lives.

When the chosen prophesy and speak to this generation, they won't have to speak using big words or eloquent language because, again, it is of God and not of them. They say what God is saying and do as He leads—no additives and no artificial colors or flavoring. This is when He starts moving. This is when His power is activated. This is when He starts shaking things up and moving upon the hearts of those He assigns us to. The apostle Paul wrote about how he operated from this place throughout his ministry:

> For Christ did not send me [as an apostle] to baptize, but [commissioned and empowered me] to preach the good news [of salvation]—not with clever and eloquent speech [as an orator], so that the cross of Christ would not be made ineffective [deprived of its saving power].
> —1 CORINTHIANS 1:17, AMP

> For they say, "His letters are weighty and forceful and impressive, but his personal presence is unimpressive and his speech contemptible [of no account]."
> —2 CORINTHIANS 10:10, AMP

The commentary notes that accompany that verse say:

> Among the Greeks, a speaker's presence and delivery were as important as his message, as the orator

Demosthenes made clear when he said that the three most important elements of a speech are delivery, delivery, and delivery. However, Paul did not follow these rules because the message of salvation does not need to be presented with fanfare in order to reach the hearts of the audience.

Then Paul shared the following in another letter to the Corinthians:

> Even though I am untrained in speech, yet I am not in knowledge. But we have been thoroughly manifested among you in all things.
> —2 CORINTHIANS 11:6

God is raising up a generation of people who will not fit the status quo, who will not come as the systems of man expect them to. Just as Jesus came, they will be of no reputation:

> [Christ Jesus] made Himself of no reputation, taking the form of a bondservant, and coming in the likeness of men. And being found in appearance as a man, He humbled Himself and became obedient to the point of death, even the death of the cross. Therefore God also has highly exalted Him and given Him the name which is above every name.
> —PHILIPPIANS 2:5–9

The chosen will be nameless and faceless. We don't have to have a name. We come in the name of the Lord and in His glory and might. We are in a time and season when all we have to do is carry on in our purpose and destiny with the awareness that the privilege of impacting is of God and not of us. Through our humility and obedience, we will be exalted so that God gets the glory He is due.

THE CHOSEN CARRY A MANTLE OF HUMILITY

We are hard-pressed on every side, yet not crushed.
—2 CORINTHIANS 4:8

The chosen have been hard-pressed. They live as those who have been through something. They are not know-it-alls and don't always have to give an opinion. They are humble and full of grace because they know where they would be without God. They are not quick to judge because they too have been pressed. When hot topics spark heated discourse on social media, you will not find the chosen spouting off. For them, if God isn't speaking, they aren't speaking. They are not trying to get brownie points from anyone. Their humility—earned from the hard seasons in their lives—keeps them in their place. They will not be pushed into saying something God did not say or doing things God didn't give them the grace to do. This keeps them secure and at peace when everyone else is striving to live up to labels and titles or popular opinions both of the church and of the world. They know what it means to be pressed by God and the cost of being chosen.

I see the chosen as a type of David. He was a man after God's heart, yet he had been hard-pressed. He was not perfect. He made terrible mistakes and decisions, but his heart was perfect toward God. He was quick to be humbled and quick to repent. These are the days when God is raising up true Davids. Davids are fearless, humble, and full of love and grace.

The chosen are hard-pressed on every side but not crushed. If you are one who desires to be chosen, know that God is coming after your emotions and your pride. He is getting ready to do some things in your life that will feel hard and unpleasant. It will be hard on your flesh, but it will be just what you need to become one who has a heart after God. The Bible says that God chastens those He loves. He prepares us to be the ones who can carry the eternal weight of glory. We must have the mantle of humility. Central to everything you do must be the awareness that the excellence of power you will walk in as a chosen one is of God and not yourself. You are an earthen vessel He has chosen to carry His glory to the ends of the earth.

THE CHOSEN ARE PEOPLE OF REVELATION

> We are perplexed, but not in despair.
> —2 CORINTHIANS 4:8

The word *perplexed* here speaks to confusion. You get this feeling when you don't know what to do. The chosen use this perplexity as fuel to push them to seek the face of the One who has all the answers. The chosen take this feeling to God, saying, "God, I don't know what to do." This is part of their humility. They won't pretend like the fakes, phonies, flimflams, and schemers, who think they know everything and are full of vanity and pride. The truth is sometimes we don't have the answer. The key here, though, is knowing who does have all the answers.

The chosen ones will have revelation. In themselves they may not have all the answers, but the spirit of revelation will rest upon their lives because they are connected to the power source. If you make the choice to live as a chosen one, you will no longer say, "I don't know what God is doing," or even, "I don't know what *I'm* doing." As a chosen one, you are a part of the revelation generation to whom God reveals Himself and His plans for those who love Him.

Glory doesn't just come all at one time. It must be revealed and uncovered as we learn who God is. So the chosen may be perplexed at times, needing revelation and clarity, but they are not in despair because they know how to get what they need. God has taught me that in times of perplexity, I need to worship. Worship brings the presence and glory of God. In His presence we begin to know Him more intimately. Our relationship with God is more valuable than all the revelation in the world. Perplexity doesn't get the chosen into despair, because the chosen know God.

THE CHOSEN ARE WORSHIPPING WARRIORS

As I just mentioned, worship brings the glory of God. I'm so hungry for the glory, and I am excited that He is raising up a generation of people who will carry His presence. God's glory comes with His presence. The two are inseparable. When we worship, we engage the presence of God and enter into a place where His glory can manifest. But not just any kind of worship will do. God is looking to pour His glory out on those who will worship Him in spirit and in truth (John 4:24). He is looking for those whose hearts are perfect toward Him (2 Chron. 16:9). It is His good pleasure to give us the kingdom (Luke 12:32), which is where His presence dwells, but many people don't want it. They want frills and fancy fixtures. They want to be connected to a club. They want to be connected to this one and that one.

What God wants, however, is a people who ultimately want to be connected to Him. He is looking for those who desire to get in His presence for real. He is separating those who come together to worship *worship* from those whose sole desire is to purely worship *Him*. He is after those who will not get lost in a song but will go deeper to tap into heaven, focusing in on God and not the worship leader.

We have to get back to truth and purity in worship. We can't have issues with idolizing what we have come to call worship. We cannot come with roaming hearts and shifty eyes. We cannot come raising hands while still overtaken by lust and perversion, as if God can't see these things—as if the condition of our hearts in His presence doesn't matter. Why? Because if we really want what we are singing and if we really want His glory to be evident in our lives, we must come with pure hearts. Sin stops the glory from flowing in your life. Do you remember Eli's sons, Hophni and Phinehas?

> Now Eli, who was very old, heard about everything his sons were doing to all Israel and how they slept with the women who served at the entrance to the tent of meeting. So he said to them, "Why do you do such things? I hear from all the people about these wicked deeds of yours. No, my sons; the report I hear spreading among the LORD's people is not good. If one person sins against another, God may mediate for the offender; but if anyone sins against the LORD, who will intercede for them?" His sons,

however, did not listen to their father's rebuke, for it was the LORD's will to put them to death.

—1 SAMUEL 2:22–25, NIV

How about Nadab and Abihu, the sons of Aaron?

Now Nadab and Abihu, the sons of Aaron, took their respective [ceremonial] censers, put fire in them, placed incense on it and offered strange (unauthorized, unacceptable) fire before the LORD, [an act] which He had not commanded them to do. And fire came out from the presence of the LORD and devoured them, and they died before the LORD.

—LEVITICUS 10:1–2, AMP

And then there is Ananias and Sapphira in the New Testament:

Now a man named Ananias, with his wife Sapphira, sold a piece of property, and with his wife's full knowledge [and complicity] he kept back some of the proceeds, bringing only a portion of it, and set it at the apostles' feet.

—ACTS 5:1–2, AMP

When Peter outed these two for conspiring together and lying about their profit, they were struck dead on the spot. The passage goes on to say that "great fear and awe gripped the whole church, and all who heard about these things" (Acts 5:11, AMP).

I am not pronouncing death on anyone, but we can clearly see from these examples that lust, disobedience, and lying cannot stand in the presence of God.

I remember one time when I was in worship with a

large group of believers. Everyone's hands were lifted up, but in the spirit I saw that some people's hands were covered in a green substance. I didn't know what it was, so I asked the Lord.

He said, "These are not clean hands."

We are in a season when we must have clean hands and a pure heart if we want to be part of the chosen ones of God, those who will carry the glory. We don't have time to play games with God and the glory He seeks to pour out on those who will represent Him well. If we are still fighting generational demons, we need to come to the altar and get right before God. Worship, prayer, and deliverance are not just things we do to be cute. We have every opportunity to be God's chosen, but we must be holy and righteous. We must be in a position to worship Him in spirit and in truth. We are Jesus lovers, and He wants us set free. Let us therefore commit and declare that we will see God's grace and glory, that every yoke will be destroyed and the anointing will be released so we can live as one of the chosen.

THE CHOSEN ARE PERSECUTED

> We are…persecuted, but not forsaken.
> —2 CORINTHIANS 4:8–9

The chosen are persecuted. They are being talked about. People wonder, "Why are they going to that conference? Why are they connected to that person? Why are they not going back to that other place?" But even though people persecute them, they are not forsaken by God. Let people talk; they are going to talk anyway. If you are a chosen one, you carry a power that is not of yourself. When you have been in the presence of God and His pleasure is your only motivation, the approval of men has no power over you. Because God desires to fill the earth with His glory, you demonstrate His power in everything you do. Because it is God's desire that no one should perish, you cast out devils. Because it is God's desire that people come to understand His great love for them, you start preaching, praying, and prophesying. You start walking in prosperity so that you can rebuild and restore the broken places in the earth.

People who don't have God's vision will always want to persecute God's chosen ones, saying things such as, "What does she think she's doing?" "How is his ministry going to grow like that?" "Did God tell her to go to the nations?" "Why did she lay hands on that person?" "Was that prophecy true?" For the last twenty years of my life, I have learned to say, "They can talk about me all they want. And I'm going to give them something to talk about." At least they are talking about the things of God!

While they are talking, I'm over in Paris bringing healing. While they are talking, I'm in Russia bringing deliverance to those who are oppressed by the devil. While they are talking, I'm in South Africa activating next-generation apostles, prophets, evangelists, teachers, and pastors. Let them talk. Let them try to raise a hand of persecution against you. But the chosen remain faithful and obedient to God because His hand is upon them.

If you want to be one of God's chosen, you must get delivered from men-pleasing spirits. You cannot be chosen and still wavering between the fear of man and the fear of God. You must choose Him every time, even in the face of persecution. God gives His chosen ones courage and clarity to be able to move forward despite heavy opposition. His glory charges, challenges, and changes them into unstoppable forces in His kingdom.

THE CHOSEN ARE DEFENDED BY GOD

The chosen face persecution, and God bears them up with His right hand to thrive despite it, but He is also their defender. More specifically the Bible says the God of Jacob defends the chosen (Ps. 20:1). What I find interesting is that the verse doesn't say, "May the God of *Israel* defend you." We know that by the time this verse was written, the author would have known that Jacob's name was changed to Israel (Gen. 32:22–32). But the verse says, "May the name of *the God of Jacob* defend you" (emphasis added). This is a powerful designation. We know that Jacob was messed up. Jacob made some mistakes. Jacob was a trickster. Jacob came from a dysfunctional family. And so many more of us can relate to the imperfect and messed-up Jacob than to the transformed Israel.

Jacob's life reads like many of our lives. Not many of us came from the Rockefeller family line. We know that if we didn't have the God of Jacob to look down upon us and defend us, we wouldn't be where we are today. The chosen are not perfect, but they have a heart after God. The chosen hold on to God for dear life and will not let go until He blesses them. This is why it is Jacob's God, and not Israel's, who defends them. God defends the chosen by giving them wisdom, and as Ecclesiastes 7:12 says, money is also a defense. He gives His chosen ones wisdom and the power to get wealth. Many times as believers we are afraid to talk about money, but the Bible says money answers all things (Eccles. 10:19). We serve a God who is known as Jehovah Jireh, which means God our Provider. We serve the God who is more than enough, the One who makes all grace abound toward us so that we'll have "all sufficiency in all things" and "abundance for every good work" (2 Cor. 9:8). But this level of abundance comes to those who follow God's principles. As we will soon see, the chosen tithe and give offerings. They help the poor and have mercy on those in need. Therefore, their finances are protected and defended by the Lord. (See Malachi 3:11.)

Then Isaiah 59:17–18 says this:

> For He put on righteousness as a breastplate, and a helmet of salvation on His head; He put on the garments of vengeance for clothing, and was clad with zeal as a cloak. According to their deeds, accordingly He will repay, fury to His adversaries, recompense to His enemies.

Let me introduce you to the God of recompense. This is God's other line of defense for His chosen ones. He is coming to destroy the enemies of their bloodline. Not only is God committed to defending the present lives of the chosen; He wants to see them and their households saved, delivered, and set free from all the power of the enemy.

Psalm 18:9 says that when God comes down from heaven on behalf of His people, He puts darkness under His feet. This says to me that God is getting ready to fight on behalf of the chosen. He is coming down ready to pay back the enemy for every attack he has put the chosen ones through. For every accusation and persecution they've experienced,

God is getting ready to release vengeance. He is releasing a new anointing that will utterly destroy the works of darkness. This eternal weight of glory that is being released will destroy the enemies that rise up against God's chosen.

THE CHOSEN KNOW NOTHING BUT JESUS CHRIST AND HIM CRUCIFIED

The chosen are determined to see the lordship of Jesus exercised over the brokenness of humanity. Jesus said that the kingdom of God dwells in us (Luke 17:21). The chosen's desire is to see the invisible kingdom manifested on earth. They desire to make the name of Jesus famous! The chosen one's core belief lies in that Jesus Christ, the Redeemer, has come and through His crucifixion has rescued us all from the enemy. Through Him we are seated in heavenly places. Through Him we see the glory of the Lord risen upon us. We stand able to be chosen because His blood makes us eligible for life at that elite status.

We don't hear Jesus and His cross of salvation preached enough. There's still redeeming power in the blood! The chosen rejoice in the blood of Jesus. Who doesn't love a good prophetic word? But if Jesus had not shed His blood on the cross, you wouldn't be able to prophesy or benefit from the prophet's gift. If He had not shed His blood on the cross, you would not be healed.

God is raising up a generation that glories in the full gospel of Jesus Christ and is determined to know nothing but Jesus Christ and Him crucified (1 Cor. 2:2).

ARE YOU CHOSEN?

This is the season when God is releasing His right hand upon a select number of people, and in His right hand there is power. In His right hand there is glory. In His right hand there is authority. In this hour God is putting His right hand of glory and authority upon the lives of His chosen ones, and He is shaking everything that can be shaken to bring about a new mantle of dominion and authority. Authority isn't authority until you use it, and it will take a whole new level of authority for God's chosen to walk in the true dominion He has destined for them.

So what do you think? Could you live life at this level—this uncompromising, God-pleasing, cross-bearing level? This is the level where people walk in the miraculous and command wealth and prosperity at such levels that they are able to restore economies and rebuild nations. This is the level where the very breath of God is on every decision, and wisdom and humility keep people positioned for success. This is the level where people walk in an unshakable level of righteousness, peace, and joy.

Do you want to be catapulted to new levels in life—financially, spiritually, and relationally? Do you want to be positioned for win after win? Do you want to see a consistent level of promotion and increase? Do you want to walk in a new level of generosity and effectiveness in your sphere of life? If so, are you ready to learn what it takes?

The chosen realm is attainable, but it is up to you to answer that call to go higher in God. As I pointed out earlier, many are called, but few are chosen. It is your response to God that determines your ability to dwell in this realm and take on this identity. The life of the chosen is holy, righteous, and set apart.

We are all called and invited into the promises of God. We all have a specific call and destiny in God. But to move from being called to being chosen, we must be ready to commit to the prerequisites in the spirit. If we want to be one of the few chosen ones, we cannot think we may just come to God any kind of way. We must give Him what He wants. He wants glory. He wants holiness. He wants righteousness. He wants purity, love, and adoration.

So choose you this day whom you will serve. The chosen are those who have unwaveringly made the choice to follow God and live in the heavenly realm. If you are ready to give God what He wants, let's go deeper into the lives of His chosen ones and see how you might be a part of that select group.

Chapter 1

THE CHOSEN REALM

...in the dispensation of the fullness of the times He might gather together in one all things in Christ, both which are in heaven and which are on earth—in Him.
—EPHESIANS 1:10

...and raised us up together, and made us sit together in the heavenly places in Christ Jesus....
—EPHESIANS 2:6

I AM CONVINCED THAT we are living in a time when God is reestablishing a divine connection between heaven and earth. He is raising up a generation that will look like heaven, and He will teach the people how to move in and out of the realms of His Spirit.

Caught in the cycles of our everyday lives, we may forget that we are spiritual beings having a natural experience. God created our bodies to house our spirits, which come alive by His very breath. Genesis 2:7 says that "the

LORD God formed [that is, created the body of] man from the dust of the ground, and breathed into his nostrils the *breath* of life; and the man became a living being [an individual complete in body and spirit]" (AMP, emphasis added).

The word *breath* in this verse is translated as "spirit."[1] God breathed His Spirit into us. The word can also mean "vital breath, divine inspiration, intellect," or "the Spirit of God imparting life and wisdom" into the soul and body of man.[2] In other words, at creation God imparted the essence of His being into us—His inspiration, intellect, life, and wisdom. All that He is has been placed in us, and by this there are things in the Spirit that He wants to manifest upon the earth through us, His beloved sons and daughters, the heirs of salvation.

As believers we maintain a level of understanding that we are created in the image of God (Gen. 1:26–28), but we do not grasp the power this reality grants us for living a supernatural, victorious, miracle-filled, dream-realizing, purpose-pursuing, and prosperous life. Because we are both spiritual and natural beings, we exist in what I call the coexisting spirit realm, where the spiritual—the unseen, intangible, heavenly, angelic, and mysterious— collides with the natural—the seen, concrete, factual, scientific, and things you can detect and know with your five senses. The coexisting realm is the place where God gathers together in one all things in Christ—things that are in heaven and things that are in the earth (Eph. 1:10). The chosen live in this realm. Allow me to clarify.

In Genesis 2:7 we learn that "the LORD God formed man of the dust of the ground, and breathed into his nostrils the breath of life; and man became a living being." When

God breathed His breath of life into Adam, He imparted to him and his infinite generations to come the ability to function in the spirit realm. The breath of life refers to life in the physical and spiritual realms. We were created to function in two worlds—the natural realm, relating to the earth, and the spiritual realm, relating to God. We are triune beings, representing the three persons of the Godhead:

1. We are spirit.

2. We possess a soul (mind, will, and emotions).

3. We live in a body.

First Thessalonians 5:23 says, "And may the God of peace Himself sanctify you through and through [separate you from profane things, make you pure and wholly consecrated to God]; and may your *spirit and soul and body* be preserved sound and complete [and found] blameless at the coming of our Lord Jesus Christ (the Messiah)" (AMPC, emphasis added).

The fall of Adam and Eve—when they disobeyed God—wasn't just a fall into sin or a mistake; it was also spiritual death. Jesus was the second Adam, sent to restore everything back to us. Therefore, the new birth experience restores to us spiritual life, which grants us the ability to operate in the natural, physical realm and the spiritual realm. Upon restoration we are spiritual babies who must learn how to exercise and develop our spiritual senses.

Partnering with a proven prophet to teach, train, and activate the gifts within you is a great way to get your spiritual senses exercised and developed. Jesus ascended on high and gave gifts to men. He gave prophets for the equipping of the saints. A major role of prophets is to train and equip believers to function in prophecy.

> And He Himself gave some to be apostles, some prophets, some evangelists, and some pastors and teachers, for the equipping of the saints for the work of ministry, for the edifying of the body of Christ.
>
> —EPHESIANS 4:11–12

Samuel, who was established and had a good report throughout Israel as a prophet of the Lord (1 Sam. 3:19–20), started schools for the prophets that provided training in things pertaining to accountability, integrity, and scriptural accuracy. The students were typically called "sons of the prophets" (1 Kings 20:35; 2 Kings 2:3, 5, 7; 4:1, 38; 9:1). Joining a church that promotes prophetic development and expression is a way to be exposed to the coexisting spirit realm and learn how to navigate within it.

For many of us, consistently making a life in this natural realm gets hard when we realize that what exists in the spirit realm is more real than the natural realm. Yet the revelation that the spiritual essence of faith actually produces something of substance and material weight is critical for the chosen ones. (See Hebrews 11:1.) We cannot live at the place God is trying to raise us up to without a firm grasp on this truth. We must believe unwaveringly that what is happening in the natural realm is temporal and only the things in the spirit realm are eternal, that things exist in the spiritual realm before they manifest on earth. For instance, there are the eternal blessings: the love of God never fails, and His mercy endures forever. If the

Bible declares that you are healed because of the stripes on Jesus' back, then you are healed.

I'll say it again: we are spiritual beings having a natural experience. God wants to release the agenda of heaven in the earth, but we will not access it if we cannot begin to really live in that chosen realm.

WHERE HEAVEN INVADES EARTH

God has an agenda, and He reveals it and delegates it to His chosen ones as they ascend to the hill of the Lord. Anytime you read in the Bible that God is calling His people to a mountain or hill, you know the agenda of heaven is about to invade earth. As one goes up to a mountain or hill, the person is ascending to higher altitudes. The person is going up to a place that is on a higher plane than what he or she normally stands on. So ascending the mountain of God represents a change in perspective or vantage point. It represents a paradigm shift or awakening. It is an invitation to go higher and think higher. It is an invitation into the mysteries of God. This is the place where God shares His secrets with His chosen ones (Amos 3:7). Being in this high place with God positions you to see things differently—to see things from His perspective and with His eyes. In this place the dream of God is revealed for the earth. The chosen ones posture their hearts to receive the invitation to change our perspective.

Too many of us are walking by sight and not by faith. We are walking by what we see in the natural and not really leaning in to see what God is pointing out to us in the spirit. We are not answering His call to come up higher and ascend His holy hill. But if we are going to choose to live as a chosen one, we need to let Him change our perspective.

To live in a realm where you are empowered to bring the things of heaven into the earth, you must have clean hands and a pure heart. The Lord says in Psalm 24:3–5:

> Who may ascend into the hill of the LORD? Or who may stand in His holy place? He who has clean hands and a pure heart, who has not lifted up his soul to an idol, nor sworn deceitfully. He shall receive blessing from the LORD, and righteousness from the God of his salvation.

The chosen have clean hands and pure hearts. They are clothed in righteousness. To dwell in the coexisting realm, we must walk in purity. The chosen realm is the coexisting spirit realm. It is the hill of the Lord—the place where the natural converges with the supernatural and the seen with the unseen. It is the place upon which we set our affections. It is a place of the "things above" and not the "things on the earth" (Col. 3:2).

The chosen have a razor-sharp focus on the things of heaven. Even with all that is happening around them, their hearts are in another place. They know they cannot afford to allow the things of earth to pull on their attention or affections and waste their strength and resources. Their hearts are set on seeing heaven manifested on earth. They are focused on seeing the kingdom expand and God's glory take over every sphere of society. Their aim is to see an end to pain, lack, brokenness, and poverty. This can only happen when they go to the hill of the Lord to receive His plans and strategies.

To see the things of the Spirit collide with earth to change everything is to understand how to live fully in this coexisting realm. Your prayers are different in the coexisting realm. Suddenly you know why Jesus taught us to pray, "Your will be done on earth as it is in heaven" (Matt. 6:10). Suddenly your word spoken in faith makes the intangible manifest as the tangible. Suddenly you are able to see that there are more with you than against you (2 Kings 6:16), as this is the realm where angels are assigned to come to our aid (Heb. 1:14). The coexisting realm is also where we can speak things that are not as though they are (Rom. 4:17).

Because the chosen understand how the spiritual and natural realms interact, they are not afraid of the enemy's resistance and they develop a relentless breakthrough spirit that brings heaven's desire on the earth. When you live in the chosen realm, you will break the church doors down to come to prayer. You will get on your knees because you will know that we access the eternal through prayer.

WHERE IT IS ALL ABOUT GOD'S POWER AND NOT OURS

> But we have this treasure in earthen vessels, that the excellence of the power may be of God, and not of us.
> —2 CORINTHIANS 4:7

I touched on this verse in the introduction. Now let's look at it in the context of what it means to live in the chosen realm. The chosen cannot afford to take credit for what God is doing. Too many people are doing this and claiming they are Spirit-filled and anointed. This cannot be.

The chosen know that the power we have—the excellence

of the power—is of God and not of us. If we understood the weight of this scripture, we would move in miracles easily. Because it is not *of* us, it is not *on* us. It's on God— the performance, the outcome, the results, or the manifestation. Living from this place is living in a position of humility before God. His working in us is all about Him and His power, not ours.

The Lord has shown me that anytime He starts moving in our hearts and releases a demonstration of His power through us, we tend to get prideful. We somehow believe we have produced these manifestations in our strength. These miracles, signs, and wonders show up because of the indwelling Holy Spirit and His power as we walk in the Spirit.

What we are seeing right now in the body of Christ is a demonstration of pride in its highest form. There is so much conceit, pride, and flesh in the pulpit. But I still believe God is going to raise up a generation that will say, "It's about Him and not me. The power you see is not mine but God's."

I understand now why William Seymour—a man very instrumental in the move of God, credited with launching the Azusa Street Revival back in the early 1900s—had so much authority in the Spirit. He was so humble and submitted to God that he would not even come from behind the two large wooden shoeboxes that served as his pulpit.[3] He wanted people to know that the power was of God and not him. Humility is the plumb line for living in the chosen realm.

As James 4:6 says, "God resists the proud, but gives grace to the humble." Grace is the empowerment of God to be kept, strengthened, and increased in our Christian faith.[4] Grace is God's "holy influence" on our lives, enabling us to grow in knowledge, affection, and the exercising of Christian virtues. Grace is the power that turns us to Christ. It is the Greek word *charis* and the root word for *charisma*, the Greek word often associated with the spiritual gifts.[5] When we are humble, God gives us power to walk in the spiritual gifts of grace—prophecy, healing, words of knowledge and wisdom, interpretation of tongues, faith, miracles, and discernment. (See 1 Corinthians 12.) When these gifts are displayed through God's chosen people, they testify of His power and might.

There are greater levels of these gifts—a greater power God wants to release that has not been released yet. He is measuring His people to see who can stand the weight of this power. Who will be able to stand up under its weight and not be destroyed by the spirit of pride? Proverbs 16:18 says, "Pride goes before destruction, and a haughty spirit before a fall." I like how *The Message* translation words it:

> First pride, then the crash—the bigger the ego, the harder the fall.

This is the same verse in The Passion Translation:

> Your boast becomes a prophecy of a future failure. The higher you lift up yourself in pride, the harder you'll fall in disgrace.

God has no desire to put His chosen ones to shame (Ps. 25:2; Isa. 54:4). He delights in our success and prosperity (Ps. 35:27). It is His will to exalt us in due season as we humble ourselves under His mighty hand (1 Pet. 5:6). He is measuring us to see if He can trust that all the glory He shines through us will be reflected back on Him.

WHERE GOD'S PROMISES
ARE YES AND AMEN

These two issues are settled in the heart of the chosen: 1) God is eternal, and 2) God is immutable. He never changes. If He said it, He is going to make good on it even when everything in the natural says something different. The chosen live on every word that proceeds out of the mouth of God (Matt. 4:4). His word is their bread of life. They know that every promise God makes to them is as good as done.

> For all the promises of God in Him are Yes, and in
> Him Amen, to the glory of God through us.
> —2 CORINTHIANS 1:20

God is the same yesterday, today, and forever. He does not change His promises. When life happens, we cannot cower in fear. We must press in and understand the promises of God. When it seems as though we are in a dry and thirsty land where there is no water, no prophetic word, no manifested blessings or answers to prayer, we must cling to the word of the Lord that says, "I change not," that says, "I am not a man that I should lie," and that says, "I am a good Father who gives good gifts to my children."

I dare you to take the promises of God, open your mouth, and declare what God has spoken over your life. Every time something traumatic happens in our lives, the devil's hope is that this time we'll keep silent. But the chosen rise up and say,

I would have lost heart, unless I had believed that I
would see the goodness of the LORD in the land of
the living. Wait on the LORD; be of good courage,
and He shall strengthen your heart; wait, I say, on
the LORD!

—PSALM 27:13–14

The chosen stay on a constant quest to know God. They
have spent time with Him, inquiring at His temple. They
are a presence generation. They value relationship with
Him over religion. Therefore, they know God is not slack
concerning His promises. Because they know Him, they
have faith in His goodness. Their hearts are strengthened
in the Lord and His unchanging character. They know
that what He says is true. They know that what they see in
the natural is not as real as what God spoke to them in the
Spirit. Therefore, they can be of good courage and wait on
Him, because He will come through.

In Exodus 3:14 God tells Moses, "I AM WHO I AM."
What does that mean? The first "I AM" means "I am here
now." Adding in the second "I AM" communicates His
omnipresence, meaning "I am here now, I am here in the
future, and I will always be here. Everything you will ever
need I am." This is also what He told Moses before he
anointed him to part the Red Sea (Exod. 14). God kept His
promise to Moses. He was I Am for the people of Israel,
and He is I Am for this chosen generation.

When we don't get these issues about God and His
promises settled in our hearts, the devil will try to push
us back. But these are the days when we had better understand the great I Am. Anything that is missing, He is. He
has been everywhere all the time. There was never a time

when God was not, and this is not changing ever. He is the God of your past, present, and future, and in the chosen realm His promises will manifest in your life.

WHERE GOD'S WISDOM IS THE PRINCIPAL THING

God's immutability (He never changes) and omniscience (He is all-knowing, never gaining or losing knowledge) are the foundation for His wisdom. He knows everything.

How long has it been said in some circles within the body of Christ that the spirit of wisdom is coming? God is saying the spirit of wisdom is here and has always been here. He knows all things. There was never a time that He did not have knowledge. What we are experiencing in this present generation—for those who come to Him and seek His face—is God downloading to us an immeasurable amount of wisdom, because all knowledge is in Him.

One of the words I've been hearing during this season is *wit* in connection with witty ideas. A witty person is one who has an "astuteness of perception or judgment" or "acumen"—discernment and insight.[6] A witty person is "a person of superior intellect"—a "thinker."[7] The person is "imaginatively perceptive and articulate."[8] Wealth generates around people like this. They are the ones who will receive from God the kind of wisdom that brings wealth.

Back when I wrote my first book, *The Prophetic Advantage*, God was revealing so much to me concerning the sevenfold spirits of God, especially the spirit of wisdom. Though I understood what He was saying to me for that time, I see it so differently now. What He has shown me is that His revelations to us contain wisdom, knowledge, and understanding. So it is not that we will just get good ideas, but He will also give us the corresponding strategy to carry them out.

I am telling you, there is a wisdom God will release by His Spirit that will bring so much wealth into the kingdom of God, but we must worship to get it. If you are not a worshipper, you will not get these downloads. The spirit of wisdom is for a presence people. It is stored up for the chosen to access.

God said, "I Am that I Am. All knowledge is in Me—all knowledge. If you don't know something, come to Me." Our human flesh leads some of us to always want to go to somebody else first before going to God, but not the chosen. The chosen know that this kind of wisdom cannot be obtained from man. First Corinthians 1:25 says that even God's foolishness—His simplest or least thought-through idea, plan, or strategy—is wiser than the best of what we can come up with on our own.

There are things right now that only exist in heaven that God wants to re-create in the earth. The chosen creators are arising, and they will access the wisdom and creativity of heaven by worshipping Elohim—the One who is the Creator.

A lot of what we think is creative now is but copycat makeover stuff. God is saying, "I'm removing the embargo off your mind, chosen one. You are going to think like Me, and you are not going to be distracted. You will bring things out of the heavenly realm into the earth realm that will bless people and increase My kingdom. Can you not see it?"

WHERE THE OMNIPRESENCE OF GOD IS THE SPIRITUAL FORCE OF THE CHOSEN

God is omnipresent. While I believe we know this in our heads, I don't think we fully grasp this attribute in terms of God's power and what is accessible to us through His omnipresence. Omnipresent means there is no place or time where or when God is not. His presence is everywhere, and He really wants us to tap into it. As I began to study the names of God, the Lord opened my mind to things about who He is that I had little experience with. Through study and revelation by His Spirit, He is showing me what various aspects of His character mean for us.

We love to say that God is the God of Abraham, Isaac, and Jacob. God says it too: "I am the God of your father—the God of Abraham, the God of Isaac, and the God of Jacob" (Exod. 3:6). But what God has shown me is that He is the God of Abraham, Isaac, and Jacob *at the same time*! He was in eternity past, *and* He is in eternity future.

When you tap into His omnipresence by His Spirit, you will be able to access future ideas, future revelation, and future strategies and bring them back into the now. Can you imagine the advantage you would have when birthing a new business, launching a ministry, writing a book, or reviving a forgotten community? You would be able to offer solutions and impact lives in ways no one has presently been able to do.

In God's omnipresence lies the power to get wealth. Wealth comes through creativity and innovation. It comes by offering something to the world that has never been seen or done before. To think that you can access the wisdom of God and bring the revelations and ideas of tomorrow into today is mind-boggling, but that is possible for the chosen. You are tapping into a spiritual force that fuels the life of God's chosen ones.

God is the Alpha and Omega at the same time. He is not Alpha today and then Omega tomorrow. No. He is both all the time. This means that when we pray for wisdom, knowledge, and understanding, we are tapping into His all-knowing, present-everywhere-at-the-same-time wisdom. When He says, "*Anything* you need, I can give it to you," He means it.

WHERE THE MANTLE OF SUPERNATURAL CREATIVITY RESTS

I hope you see why I am calling the chosen a presence people. The devil knows the value of God's presence. He knows what we gain from dwelling there. He comes after our relationship with God to destroy the connection that is the source of God's power in the earth. We are the glory carriers. We are the ones through which God changes and transforms lives.

The devil is against God, His creation, and everything righteous and good. Therefore, he tries to keep us from the power of God's presence by making us think we are nothing. He uses insecurity and unworthiness to keep us from going to God in prayer, Bible study, and worship. As long as he wins this battle, demonic strongholds like rejection and poverty will keep us bound and from living out our highest potential.

Yet God is moving on our behalf. He is tearing down religious systems and structures that want to keep us out of His presence. His presence is where His glory is. His glory is where His power lies. We need access to His glory to be empowered to do all He has designed us to do. There is no limit to the ways and means by which these things will manifest.

God is releasing a mantle of creativity that will include supernatural healing in the form of re-creation of limbs and organs such as kidneys and livers. People are on waiting lists for months and years for these essential organs. They cannot live without them. But our all-powerful God is manifesting Himself once again as the Creator.

We know how to worship Him as Jehovah Jireh, our provider—especially in the American church—but do we know how to worship Him as Elohim, the Creator of heaven, earth, and everything in between? The One who can create eyes and limbs is the same One who can release a whole new level of creativity for miracles, provision, wealth, and so much more.

Harnessing this understanding brings a whole new meaning to Philippians 2:5: "Let this mind be in you which was also in Christ Jesus." Have we not read about Jesus miraculously healing and restoring function to nerves, muscles, and bones? What do we think happened on the inside of Bartimaeus' body when Jesus restored his sight? (See Mark 10:46–52.) What happened to the bones and muscles of the lame man who got up and walked after thirty-eight years (John 5:1–4), or the nerves in the man's once withered hand (Mark 3:1–6)? The men received new internal physical structures that allowed their once dysfunctional organs to be made new and to work again.

This is the level of miraculous creativity that the chosen are to bring down from the heavenly realm into the earthly realm. Yes, this creative power and glory even extends to inventions and witty ideas, as I mentioned before. We must see that even ideas restore lives and reshape the world.

God is going to take us—His chosen—into the future where we will see things like we've never seen them before. Prepare now for it.

WHERE THE TRUE PROPHETIC IS ABOUT SUBSTANCE

We are talking about a real prophetic advantage when we get into the chosen realm. You must be able to understand what it means that God is the same yesterday, today, and forever.

In reality God doesn't prophesy. Think about it. If He is present simultaneously in the past, present, and future, what lies in the future is like what is present for Him. He prophesies from your future, but since He is there now as much as He is in your present, can He really be prophesying?

Have you ever seen someone get a prophetic word and thought, "Oh, the prophet missed it. He is way off with that one. That can't be this person"? What you heard just didn't seem possible based on what you knew about the person right then. But let me tell you, a true prophet will unveil who a person is even into the future because a true prophet sees what God sees.

If someone is "prophesying" to you based on who you were in the past, the person is operating under the influence of a familiar spirit. The enemy is always using our past against us, while God is always leading us to press in to the things that are ahead (Phil. 3:13–14). True prophets will look into your future and see what God is saying. He or she will look into the creative force of God and, by the power of the Word, send you there.

We may know all these things about God with our heads, but they need to become a functioning part of our spiritual beings. God is getting ready to test some things in you because there are things the Lord wants to get out of you so they can be released in the earth. You may say, "Lord, I'm sorry. I don't have that anointing today." But He goes into your future and pulls from the power you will mature into and says, "Here. Take it. Here is the anointing you need right here." In Him we have everything we need— nothing is missing; nothing is lacking; nothing is broken.

There were times when we trivialized the power of God by telling people to touch five people and say this or that, run around, touch the ground, do the hokey pokey, and turn yourself around. That is *not* what it is all about. That is Christian charismatic witchcraft. A new generation is arising, and we want substance. We want to know God. We want to know how to live in a way that pleases Him so that we will remain welcomed in His presence. Vain decrees and declarations—we're over them. We're over prophesying to the wind and things not changing. There must be something greater and bigger going on—and there is. The chosen are living it.

WHERE THE PRIVILEGE TO BEAR THE WEIGHT OF GLORY COSTS YOU SOMETHING

Now here we come to the foundational Scripture passage for the chosen lifestyle and the chosen realm: 2 Corinthians 4:7–17. I've already quoted parts of it in the introduction and throughout this chapter. I will quote it here in its entirety, and you will come across it again as we continue this journey to discovering what it means to be not only called but chosen.

The passage reads:

> But we have this treasure in earthen vessels, that the excellence of the power may be of God and not of us. We are hard-pressed on every side, yet not crushed; we are perplexed, but not in despair; persecuted, but not forsaken; struck down, but not destroyed—always carrying about in the body the dying of the Lord Jesus, that the life of Jesus also may be manifested in our body. For we who live are always delivered to death for Jesus' sake, that the life of Jesus also may be manifested in our mortal flesh. So then death is working in us, but life in you.
>
> And since we have the same spirit of faith, according to what is written, "I believed and therefore I spoke," we also believe and therefore speak, knowing that He who raised up the Lord Jesus will also raise us up with Jesus, and will present us with you. For all things are for your sakes, that grace, having spread through the many, may cause thanksgiving to abound to the glory of God.
>
> Therefore we do not lose heart. Even though our outward man is perishing, yet the inward man is being renewed day by day. For our light affliction, which is but for a moment, is working for us a far more exceeding and eternal weight of glory.

I used to meditate on this and shout. I used to just teach on the eternal weight of glory. Oh, I remember how I cried out, "God, I want the eternal weight of glory!" Then something happened. God started answering my prayers with pressure. I'm talking about like ten years of pressure, and I didn't understand it.

I said, "Lord, what is all this pressure and testing about? What else do You desire of me?" I have been serving the Lord since I was twenty-four. No missteps and no here today and gone tomorrow. None of that is part of my story. But when I started decreeing this scripture over my life, there came a vicious attack from the enemy as if I had opened some doors to him. God showed me there were treasures still inside of me that He wanted to release through me. So I had to learn how to stand under pressure, which was the weight of God's glory pushing and pulling greatness out of me. In the process, I had to go through a breaking of my flesh. And it was through this process that I authored nine or ten books and traveled to more than fifty-five nations preaching the gospel of Jesus Christ. Please understand that I am making my boast in the Lord. The excellency of the power of God in my life is of Him and not me.

We are seeing people rise quickly to prominence within the body of Christ. They become Facebook phenoms with thousands of followers overnight, people who are really copying what they have heard from more seasoned saints— prophets and apostles, pastors and teachers who have paid the price—and preaching it as if it were their own. But in our microwave culture, people hardly notice. They are caught up in the sensation and the momentary feeling. Yet in the heavenlies it is evident that these "phenoms" have no weight.

I don't believe God will let this continue for long, because a generation that wants more is arising. This is a people who are desperate for the presence and power of God. We will carry the weight of glory.

I don't know about you, but I want to speak and see heaven move. I want to declare and see angels move. I am not concerned about moving people, because people are fickle. People will say they love you one day, and the next day they will curse you. God is delivering us from desiring people's approval and seeking their opinions. God wants to cut the puppet strings that cause us to depend on the systems of man.

The wealth transfer that is coming is not just about our acquisition of material things. It is to break our reliance on man-made systems. God wants no nation, government, bank, or ungodly board of trustees to control our access to what rightfully belongs in the hands of His chosen ones. God wants everything we get to come from Him.

I pray that the enemy loose your mind concerning money and finances. We have been tricked and bound by the enemy to deify and hallow poverty. Poverty is not part of the kingdom of God for very strategic purposes. The Bible says that poverty is one of the things Jesus took on Himself at the cross so that we would be made rich (2 Cor. 8:9). In the chosen realm money answers all things (Eccles. 10:19).

We must learn to bear the pressure. Second Corinthians 4:8 says that "we are hard-pressed on every side, yet not crushed." The enemy wants us to feel crushed so we give up our resolve to serve Jesus and His kingdom. So what does he do? He begins to release stuff against our lives.

Four days before my 2017 Chosen conference my stepson committed suicide. My emotions were everywhere. I wondered what the meaning of it all was. I wanted to give up. But God sent reinforcements. He worked on my emotions and strengthened me from the inside out. He helped me to see that I was pressed but not crushed. If I had given in to the enemy and believed that all was lost, that I was crushed and broken beyond repair, I would have given up. But these are the days when we cannot afford to let our emotions control us. If we don't feel happy, we stop going to church. Or if we're angry, we cut someone off in traffic or curse them out at the bank. If we feel lonely and entitled, we may give in to lust when that fine young thing passes in front of our eyes.

But in the chosen realm—where we abide under the weight of glory—fear, anger, hopelessness, lust, and any other dangerous emotions are pressed out of us. God's people cannot be moved by their emotions.

When we get into these situations and our emotions are out of control, we need to be truthful with the Lord. Don't put on a religious mask. Let Him send reinforcements from heaven to bear you up. Get before Him and repent.

You cannot move in the things of God in this hour with all kinds of anger, bitterness, and unforgiveness. You are not going to carry the glory of God with those things in your heart.

These are the days when there will be no mixture. God is looking for a righteous people. He is looking for a whole people. He is looking for those who will carry His glory, so He allows the pressures to come.

In these times of great temptation you are given an opportunity to truly set your affections on things above because it is going to take a spiritually minded people to fulfill the kingdom mandate. I have learned to thank God for the pressure, as Paul suggests in 2 Corinthians 4:16–17.

Without it we would not be in a position to carry His glory or live in the chosen realm.

The appointment to becoming a chosen one is not anything we can take lightly. There is a cost. As God sets you on the path to living as one of His chosen, I want to encourage you not to be afraid to step up and enter into the chosen realm. It is a place of God's design just for you. It is the coexisting realm where the things of heaven manifest on earth, the unseen becomes seen, and the supernatural collides with the natural.

In order to withstand the transition, you must strip yourself before the Lord. Be honest with Him. Let Him heal your emotions and build an unshakable faith within you. Then, when the time comes for you to be released in the fullness of what it means to be chosen, you will have the confidence to know that as you step out, the full power of every attribute contained within the person of God is available to you.

Chapter 2

THE PATH OF THE CHOSEN

You will show me the path of life; in Your
presence is fullness of joy; at Your right
hand are pleasures forevermore.
—PSALM 16:11

ANY OF US today have taken on the expectations of the microwave culture we are living in. We even have microwave Christianity. We want things in an instant. We want them now. That's why some put so much value in actions that make religion all about what we can get quickly. If we don't get it when we want it, we lose faith and feel that God is not for us. But God wants to show us that being chosen is about the journey. We are set on a path of ever-increasing righteousness, holiness, joy, abundance, favor, and wisdom. We don't arrive at a destination in the chosen life. Living things grow. Dead things do not.

God is committed to our growth. Growth does not

happen instantaneously. It happens over time. The path of life is a journey to growing in God so that what He wants to develop in us will bear eternal fruit—fruit that will last (John 15:16). There is treasure in us that He wants to pull out. How does God get treasure out of our earthen vessels? Through testing and training along the path of life. The treasure is our call, our purpose, our gift, or our measure of influence. It is our eternal weight of glory, and for it to come out, we must be willing to walk this journey with God. We must walk with God along the path of life He has laid out for us.

Again, God is committed to your growth. It is not His will that you have a gift and no clarity—a gift and no maturity.

Proverbs 4:18 says that the path of the just, or the chosen, is a path of life and righteousness that just gets brighter and brighter. God is saying that these are days when there is a people He wants to bless. These are days when, as a chosen one, you will enter into the greatest times of blessing, but you must get on the path God has designed you to be on. It is a righteous path. God is saying, "I'm raising up people with righteous hearts."

Our society is hungry. It's like it's going crazy because people don't understand what righteousness is. They are trying to redefine things with their own finite views without seeking God, who knows all. The lack of foundation and compromised standards have seeped into the body of Christ. But I believe we are in a season where God is purifying our motives. He is setting us straight with what pleases Him and allowing us to walk in favor with both God and man. He has given His chosen ones divine instructions, and because we love Him and His presence, we are going to go after it. We will pursue Him on the path He has laid out for us. We're going to be on the hunt to build and make the name of Jesus famous again.

Proverbs 3 is my go-to resource for what it takes to remain securely on the chosen path, which includes:

- Trusting in the Lord: "Trust in the LORD with all your heart, and lean not on your own understanding; in all your ways acknowledge Him, and He shall direct your paths" (Prov. 3:5–6).

- Fearing the Lord: "Do not be wise in your own eyes; fear the LORD and depart from evil. It will be health to your flesh, and strength to your bones" (Prov. 3:7–8).

- Honoring the Lord: "Honor the LORD with your possessions, and with the firstfruits of all your increase; so your barns will be filled with plenty, and your vats will overflow with new wine" (Prov. 3:9–10).

- Keeping God as your confidence: "When you lie down, you will not be afraid; yes, you will lie down and your sleep will be sweet. Do not be afraid of sudden terror, nor of trouble from the wicked when it comes; for the LORD will be your confidence, and will keep your foot from being caught" (Prov. 3:24–26). Fear will cause you to stumble. Fear breeds desperation. Fear will lead to your emotions being all over the place. The Lord will send His Spirit to strengthen and stabilize you. The Lord is your confidence, your foundation, your cornerstone, and your strong tower.

- Walking in kindness and generosity: "Do not withhold good from those to whom it is due, when it is in the power of your hand to do so" (Prov. 3:27).

- Avoiding the curse of the Lord: "The curse of the LORD is on the house of the wicked, but He blesses the home of the just" (Prov. 3:33).

- Remaining humble: "Surely He scorns the scornful, but gives grace to the humble" (Prov. 3:34)

Proverbs 3 contains a few more points that are critical to our understanding as we journey with God along the path of the chosen. Let's take a closer look now at what they are.

ALLOW GOD TO CHASTEN YOU

My son, do not despise the chastening of the LORD, nor detest His correction; for whom the LORD loves He corrects, just as a father the son in whom he delights.

—PROVERBS 3:11–12

As I've said earlier, the Lord is committed to our growth, and if we want to grow, we have to be open to correction when we get something wrong.

The Bible says that God chastens those He loves. God

loves His chosen ones, and they get the exclusive benefit of the Lord's chastening and discipline. The chastening of God brings about holiness, transformation, deliverance, and cleansing from idolatry, unfaithfulness, iniquity, and bloodline curses.

I have experienced God's chastening in my own life and still do to this day. I am so grateful for it. One time I was called to another country to minister with a group of other prophets. If I recall correctly, I was the only woman, and I was cute too. I had on a red suit and some animal-print heels. I was ready. I knew what the Lord had been stirring in me, and if I was let loose, I knew the fire of God would fall. But the men were more experienced and well known, so I wasn't given any preference.

As the prophetic ministry went forth and the men prophesied with authority and stepped up to the front to speak, I kept getting pushed further and further to the back of the stage. I'm little, and I know I could not be seen. I just moved myself to the back and tried to stay out of the way. God was telling me to just stand there and be silent. I was like, "God, did I do something wrong? Why are You putting me on the bench?" But I obeyed, even as I felt the prophetic temperature in the room reach a certain point where I knew they wanted breakthrough. As a prophet of God, I must obey Him first and not get into wanting to be seen or heard. He told me to stand there and be quiet.

Just as I thought things were winding down and it was my time to go sit down, one of the leaders remembered I was there, called me to the front, and asked if I had a word. Yes, I did. I said what God had been speaking to me for the people there, and the room erupted with the glory of

God. Deliverance, healings, miracles, and more happened right there.

If I had not listened to God, I don't know what witness I would have given another woman who was watching and learning how to operate in predominantly male spaces. If I had not listened to God and tried to grab a mic and prophesy without His permission, I would have been in the flesh, and there's no telling the damage my ego and disobedience could have caused. I love to prophesy, and I love to preach, but God continues to train me and soften my heart to be in complete submission to Him. We cannot be part of God's chosen if we will not obey Him and stay open to His chastening.

Another time God used one of His prophets to speak into my life. Kevin Leal has served as a type of Mordecai in my life, keeping me in line with my unique call. He used to slap me on my back and say, "Prophesy, girl!" He told me, "With the anointing that is on your life, you must always stay feminine. Keep your perfume. Wear your dresses." He told me that I must not try to be like a man in ministry, "though some may be intimidated by the anointing that is on your life. Your voice is big. Let God do it," he said. And this was all stated in brotherly love by a senior in the faith and a prophetic mentor. God sends these types of people into our lives to keep us on the path He has uniquely designed for us.

The power of submission is phenomenal. So many people who were supposed to be Apostle John Eckhardt's friend, people who knew he was my mentor and that I served in his ministry for years, tried to get me to come and work with them. I don't even think he knew. "Come over here and work with us," they would say.

"Look, I am not a hireling," I would think, "and I have been delivered from the orphan spirit. I have a home."

The chastening of God brings deliverance from areas of weakness that could cause us to sabotage our walk with Him. When you have an orphan spirit and don't get delivered from it, you will operate as if you have no father, and anyone will be able to pull you away because you don't have a covenant heart. God wants to break any residue of the orphan spirit off the lives of His chosen people. So many of us are looking for a father or mother, but we have a heavenly Father first. We'll talk more about breaking free of the orphan spirit in chapter 6. But for now I want to remind you that whether you were raised by only one parent or neither parent, you have a heavenly Father. The next step, as you grow into this understanding, is becoming a good son or daughter.

The devil doesn't know everything you were called to do, but he is familiar with your bloodline. For some women, he may think, "On this bloodline there are strong women leaders, so I will assign the opposite—the spirit of Jezebel and rejection (a door opener). And then I'm going to assign men with the spirit of Ahab in her life so they can connect and abort the called."

But then God releases His grace and mercy through chastening and through mentorship from the saints—He is always working to get us to our destiny. He is committed to our growth.

God was the One who got this party started. He loved us first. He chose us first. God initiated this, and He is faithful to complete everything He started in us. So that your joy may be complete, allow God to chasten you, teach you, and discipline you. He wants to free you from all kinds of things that will pervert the purity of the anointing on your life, for He desires clean hands and a pure heart.

FIND WISDOM; GAIN UNDERSTANDING

> Happy is the man who finds wisdom, and the man who gains understanding.
>
> —PROVERBS 3:13

Wisdom is the principal thing. It helps you to walk safely on the path and keeps you from stumbling (v. 23). These are days when the Lord is releasing fresh wind. He is releasing wisdom and revelation over your life as you've never known it before. He said, "I want My people to understand that I am the King of glory. I am the Lord, mighty in battle."

Anytime you are moving forward in God, there is potential for spiritual war. Why? Because sometimes you are moving into and taking over territory occupied by the enemy. There are times in the chosen life when confronting the enemy and overcoming adversity are unavoidable, and you need wisdom to help you navigate the uncharted land. At some turns or crossroads in the journey, circumstances may seem insurmountable. You may be overwhelmed at times, feeling as if you aren't qualified for the next level. Decisions are harder. More people need the gifts and talents you possess. You will need wisdom. "If any man lacks wisdom, let him ask of God..." (Jas. 1:5).

Solomon's first prayer to God after becoming king of Israel was for wisdom to lead and serve well in his new assignment. He received it in abundance as well as immeasurable wealth. Moses, a reluctant leader at first, received wise counsel from his father-in-law, who told him how to delegate the leadership responsibilities among able men of God so he wouldn't have to bear the burdens of the growing nation alone (Exod. 18:1–23).

Wisdom is there for us at each level God brings us to. As the chosen ones we must press in to God and get the wisdom we need for this hour.

> The wise shall inherit glory, but shame shall be the legacy of fools.
>
> —Proverbs 3:35

REMAIN PURE AND UPRIGHT

> For the perverse person is an abomination to the Lord, but His secret counsel is with the upright.
>
> —Proverbs 3:32

The word *perverse* here not only is used in relation to sexual perversion, as we are quick to assume based on some teachings in our churches. It also means "to depart" or "turn aside," "to go wrong, go crooked," "to go back," or just plain "wickedness."[1] Perversion is about walking away from God. It is being "turned away from what is right or good: corrupt" and "obstinate in opposing what is right, reasonable, or accepted."[2] When our hearts are perverse, we will not have the secret counsel of the Lord. The chosen thrive off the counsel and revelation of God. We cannot live without it. Because we know our need for His counsel, we seek to maintain a pure and upright heart before the Lord.

God has been really speaking to me out of Psalm 24. As I studied, prayed through, and ministered this *chosen* message, I kept hearing, "Who may ascend the hill of the Lord?"

As I said in the introduction, anytime in Scripture you read where God was calling people to meet Him on a hill or mountain, those were places He designated for His people to encounter Him. So in Psalm 24 God was saying, "Who are those who can encounter Me?" We get an immediate answer: "He who has clean hands and a pure heart" (v. 4).

God is calling out to His chosen ones, "Who are the ones who can stand in My presence, hear My instruction, and bring it to a generation who needs to hear the purity of My voice? Who will represent Me?"

I believe we are in a season when those in this generation need to hear the purity of the voice of the Lord. We are in a time when they need leaders—men and women of God—to rise up with a pure message and clean hearts.

What does it mean to have clean hands? It means having integrity. Hands represent motives or works. We must allow God to purify our motives and works in order to remain on the path of life and move in great power and strength. As He purifies us, He is increasing our capacity to handle more authority. When you get real power, authority, and even wealth in your life, they reveal who you are. God wants to make sure that as you come in His name, what is revealed is pure.

In the next part of verse 4 the Lord says this: "who has not lifted up his soul to an idol, nor sworn deceitfully." Now we get a better understanding of what it means to be impure or perverse in God's eyes. As we just saw, perversion is related to departing from God, going the wrong way, or turning away. When we put other things above God and give them our allegiance and worship, we are walking in idolatry. We are turning away from God and giving first place to something other than God. The spirit of idolatry—namely personality idolatry—is one of the major things God is rooting out of the body of Christ. Sometimes we get so caught up in personalities and people and movements that we forget to put Jesus first. I believe these are days when God is removing all idolatry out of our lives as we ascend the hill of the Lord.

God is giving His chosen ones new instructions in this hour, and the reason we sometimes don't fulfill what God tells us to do is we have wrong allegiances. On the path of life God is correcting and rebalancing our allegiances. He is ridding us of all idolatry, lust, and perversion. Anything in your heart that stops you from obeying the will of God is an idol. Anything you have more faith in than you do in God is an idol. God requires pure and uncompromised devotion from us. Nothing less.

One of these idols is fear. Listen, beloved. Fear is really a false expectation appearing real. You may have heard it a different way—that fear is false evidence appearing real—but I want to show you something. Fear, for most of us, is about what we expect in the future. Expectation is "a strong belief that something *will* happen or will be the case;" "a belief that someone *will* or should achieve something."[3] We are afraid about what will not turn out well in the future.

When you let this kind of fear outweigh God—who is more than enough; who is your provider; who protects; who is your healer; who is omnipotent and omnipresent; who is the same yesterday, today, and forever—you are saying that tomorrow's problems or issues are bigger than God. Sometimes when you measure the fear in your life, you may find that you have an idol. You are giving more weight and value in your life to fear than you are to God.

And I believe these are days when God is removing all idolatry and falsehoods out of our lives. He must because His plan is to raise up a people who have clean hands and pure hearts and are sold out completely to Him.

The chosen are those who pledge their allegiance to the Lamb of God and not to any personality's or organization's brand—not to any movement but to the kingdom of God. We are a generation set on the path of life and will not lose our focus on Him. We will not be everywhere doing everything, but we will pursue the thing God has assigned us to do.

Do not allow your soul to be lifted up to an idol. Truly seek the face of God. Accept His invitation to walk the path of life and ascend to His holy hill, where He will tell you secret things you do not know, where He will give you divine wisdom and strategy. Do not allow yourself to be taken by ego and cast from His presence. Again, the excellency of His power is not of us; it is of Him. Pride is a form of idolatry where we place ourselves and our needs above God. He is purifying us of everything that would get in the way of our staying on the path He ordained for us.

HOW TO FIND YOUR PATH

When you accepted Christ, you came off the path of destruction and God rerouted you onto the path of life. As Ephesians 2:2 says, "You once walked according to the course of this world." The same Spirit who made you "alive together with Christ" and seated you "in the heavenly places" will also lead you onto the course of heaven uniquely designed for you.

In speaking His plans for our lives, God works through

the prophetic anointing, which is why the chosen are presence people. In the presence of God we can hear what He is saying; we can speak it forth and begin to see things line up, showing us which way to go. The Bible says that as you come out of the path of adversity and affliction, "your teachers will not be moved into a corner anymore, but your eyes shall see your teachers. Your ears shall hear a word behind you, saying, 'This is the way, walk in it,' whenever you turn to the right hand or whenever you turn to the left" (Isa. 30:20–21).

Sometimes those teachers are the prophets God sends to speak a word of revelation over your life. Other times it is your ear and your spirit tuned in to the Spirit Himself that allows revelation to lead you in the way you should go.

Many people have come to me, saying, "Prophetess, I know God loves me, but I don't know what I should be doing." The Word of God contains the will of God, but it is through your personal relationship with Him that the Lord reveals the specifics of your life. Trust that when your desires and thoughts have been purified and made holy, whatever you feel in your heart to do is what God is telling you to do. Start speaking it out loud, start making declarations, and pray for instructions and strategy. As you pray and declare what God has spoken to your heart to do, the grace of God will fall upon your life. The heavens will open over your life, and know that the power, favor, strength, and glory of God is coming.

You will know it by revelation.

The chosen are of the revelation generation because they are a presence people. You will hear this again and again. The chosen cannot thrive outside the presence of God.

His Word is a lamp to our feet and a light to our path (Ps. 119:105). Light is symbolic of spiritual revelation or enlightenment. No longer will we say we don't know what we are doing. The path of God is illuminated, revealed, and uncovered step by step over time. Jesus promised that when the Holy Spirit, who is also the Spirit of truth, came, He would reveal all things regarding our lives to us.

Revelation brings understanding and interpretation.

See, many of us are in the same place we've been for a while. We are stagnant because we need interpretation. Prophetic revelation brings interpretation. If you are like many believers, you have gotten a lot of downloads, but you have little understanding about what they mean for your life and how you can move forward in them. God will give you instructions and patterns on how you can advance forward. It may come by the man or woman of God, or God may speak to you directly. He will show you how to tap into the dreams of your heart, which is important because the course of your life is charted by the dreams of your heart, if they've been sanctified. God moves in your heart through desire; that is why Scripture says He will give you the desires of your heart if you delight yourself in Him (Ps. 37:4).

You will be led on your path of life by His presence.

Hungering for the presence of God is more than just wanting to be in wonderful worship at a great church. In church or out, in everyday life up against everyday circumstances and choices, God is causing us to become people of His presence. If we are going to know how to fulfill our purpose and destiny, we must hunger for His presence more than anything else. God guides by His presence. We must become like the people of Israel, a people who follow the cloud by day and the fire by night. We must become those who ask God to teach us and allow Him to lead us in the way we should go.

Praying, worshipping, studying the Bible, meditating, and fasting when it's necessary are keys to remaining in the presence of God. The more we stay in His presence, the more familiar we become with Him and His voice. Jesus said, "My sheep hear My voice" (John 10:27). The word *hear* in this context not only is about our physical senses but is also about following and obeying what we hear. "I know them, and they follow Me" (v. 27).

God will reveal to you the path of life. He will lay it out before you and illuminate it with His Word. You are then responsible for doing as He has spoken.

Just as we are likened to sheep, we are also called sons. The Scripture tells us that the sons of God are led by the Spirit of God (Rom. 8:14). We have to return sonship back to the body of Christ. We're not just members. We are sons and daughters of the living God, and we are to be led by His presence.

The one thing that distinguishes disciples of the Lord Jesus Christ from followers of any other religion is that we serve the true and living God. And if God is alive in us, then His presence should be with us. It is not just about being gifted; we also have to be anointed. We want to be called, but even more than that we want to be chosen. We want to be gifted *and* anointed. We want the very presence of God. The earmark is if God is with you, then His presence should be with you. His presence, His essence, His divine nature should be resting upon your life.

When you are on the path of life with God, He transforms you by His presence and you begin to see yourself in the light of what He made you.

GOD IS FIGHTING FOR YOU TO REMAIN ON YOUR PATH

Psalm 24:7–8 says, "Lift up your heads, O ye gates; and be ye lift up, ye everlasting doors; and the King of glory shall come in. Who is this King of glory? The LORD strong and mighty, the LORD mighty in battle" (KJV). This passage reveals that the Lord will cause His name—King of glory—to be lifted up and praised in the earth. This is the day when God is releasing such a great revelation, or revealing, of His glory—the very nature of who He is, which is reflected in you. And so He wants you to know that He is fighting for you. He is your Lord, mighty in battle, and He is fighting for you and the things He has placed in your heart to pursue.

We will talk about this throughout this book, but I will say it here as well: God is releasing angels assigned to your destiny, and they will help you stay on the path of life. The Holy Spirit is here with you as well, bringing you revelation about what it is you are here on earth to do. Every resource of heaven is dispatched to you as you remain on the path.

I think it is so phenomenal, so majestic, to know that we have the indwelling Spirit—the *Holy Spirit*—living in us! Jesus said, "Listen. I am going away, but I will not leave you comfortless. I'm going to send you One even greater than Myself, and He will teach you everything. He will be with you." (See John 14:26.)

Beloved, you are not in the world by chance. You are not in this decade by chance. God has a purpose and a plan for your life, and He is going to send everything you need to fulfill the purpose within His greater purpose, that which He created you for. But you must ascend the hill of the Lord. Ascending the hill of the Lord is going up into a place to be with God. You set and discipline your affections on things above.

He wants you to see clearly the reality of the coexisting spiritual realm so you know without a shadow of a doubt that there truly is so much help for you. With God and heaven on your side, you are the majority. Just as Elisha said to Gehazi in the heat of battle, "Do not fear, for those who are with us are more than those who are with them" (2 Kings 6:16).

The host of heaven are waiting to assist you. They are rooting for you to fulfill your destiny. They are waiting for you to connect, to activate them, and to call on them and give the command. They are waiting for you to bind things and to call miracles and wonders forth that are not currently in the earth or natural realm. They want to see God's power and glory manifested through your life just as much as you do.

God is saying that these are days in which the fullness of who you are is going to arise. And once we understand and see ourselves as God sees us, beloved, we are going to be some of the happiest people. We are going to be filled with the joy of the Lord. Our families will be made whole, and we will cause all the families of the earth to be blessed.

What did He tell Abraham? He said, "Through you all the families of the earth are going to be blessed." So I am decreeing that we begin to understand who we are and align with God to walk with Him on the path He has uniquely ordained for us. Families will be blessed by what you do *and* what you *don't* do. Our response to God's invitation to walk with Him on this path and to remain faithful is critical. We say this a lot in the body of Christ, but it is true: there are people attached to your gifts and anointing. And how we stay clean and pure before God determines the effectiveness of those gifts and anointings.

We must understand the weight of glory that we carry. We are representatives of the King of kings. We have been put here to manifest the kingdom of God. To help us and to strengthen our faith in His love toward us, He declares to us that He is the God who is mighty in battle. Again, He wants you to understand that He is fighting for you. He never loses. God never, ever loses. All He does is win. As a matter of fact, God has already won. This is why the chosen must set their affections on things above. The stuff happening around us and the things that try our faith will tell us something different. But as I have said, the things in the spiritual realm are more real and eternal than the things in the natural realm. We need to discipline what we set our eyes on so we are not distracted or discouraged and do not leave the path God has set us on.

Now let's talk about our set times and appointments on the chosen path.

Chapter 3

CHOSEN TIMES
AND APPOINTMENTS

And He has made from one blood every nation of men to dwell on all the face of the earth, and has determined their preappointed times and the boundaries of their dwellings.
—ACTS 17:26

A S WE ARISE in our chosen identity and destiny, we must understand the role that timing plays. There is a special and specific timing for every purpose to be revealed for the advancing of the kingdom. As we seek God for revelation of His plan for our lives and ask that He illuminate our paths, we need to include prayers that will help us enter into the set time of God.

The Bible mentions two key words for time, *chronos* and *kairos*. Chronos is everyday time—one o'clock, two o'clock, Monday, Tuesday, Wednesday, and the like. It's routine, daily time. It's "time either long or short."[1] What we do with chronos—our everyday lives, our routine time—and how we spend our days, moments, and seconds affect when we step into the other level of time, which is called kairos—a set time, a time God has appointed for you to walk in your destiny. Kairos is the time when God opens up opportunity—"the right time," the "set or proper time," the "opportune or seasonable time," or a "definite time."[2]

You may have a passion, dream, or vision, but what you do with your chronos time (your everyday life) prepares the platform for the set time. There's a set time for you to launch your ministry, start your business, hold your conference, or publish your book. The path, purpose, and passion of the chosen are governed by the convergence of chronos time with kairos time.

I first got the prophetic word that I would write books on October 16, 1996. Then, on the same date two years later, in 1998, I got another word that I would write books, and they would be a major part of my income. Do you know that my first book, *The Prophetic Advantage*, wasn't published until October 12, 2012? Sixteen years passed between the time I received the first word and the set time for the book to be published.

Between chronos time and set time is the time when God prepares your life to shoulder the weight of His glory you will carry in the appointed season. Everything in *The Prophetic Advantage*, everything in this book, and everything in the books I wrote between the first book and the most recent one is all that I learned, walked through, and experienced. What I write isn't just head knowledge. The words and lessons I share have come from my life. When I first received a prophetic word all the way to becoming a prophet and traveling to nations covered a span of sixteen years that God used to prepare me for what would come forth as an author.

Though much of what we access as chosen ones comes from the spiritual world, God trains us in the natural. Our natural understanding and natural wisdom are super-charged by God's infinite wisdom and omniscience.

The devil tries to make us impatient and do things in our natural lives that will throw us off timing and lead to a cycle of defeat. His goal is to get to us before the timing of God approaches. We have to pray in this hour for God to guard our times and seasons because we do not want to be ahead of God, nor do we want to be behind God. We want God to synchronize our lives with the time clock of heaven so that we are in the right place at the right time with the right people doing the right thing, fulfilling our destiny.

Who you are today is the sum total of what you have done with your time. There is nothing more important than time and how you spend it. Don't waste time. Every moment and every day you have are important to God. Time is the measure of life. You must make sure to do the right things with your time.

NUMBERING OUR DAYS

So teach us to number our days, that we may gain a heart of wisdom.

—PSALM 90:12

The Bible tells us in Ecclesiastes 3:1–8 that there is a time and season for everything: a time to be born and a time to die, a time to laugh and a time to cry. There is even a time to rest. There is a time for everything. Whatever you do, make sure you are doing it according to the timing of God. What you do today will affect your tomorrow, so ask God to teach you to number your days so you may gain a heart of wisdom. In plain speech, this means we need to learn how to use our time.

Think about this: If you had another ten years on this side of eternity, what would you want to do with those next ten years of life? When we speak about life in terms of years—ten years, for example—it sounds as if you have forever. But when we put it in terms of days, ten years is only 3,650 days. If you have another twenty years, then that's 7,300 days. That doesn't sound like a lot of time, now does it? That's why we read the prayer from the psalmist, saying, "Teach us to number our days." They may have had a revelation that they really didn't have that much time left to live their lives and fulfill God's plan and purpose for them.

So I encourage you not to think of your life in terms of years; think in days. God always wants us to think in days. Begin to order your life by the day. Set up your day; order your day. I think the best thing you can do is get up in the morning, seek God through prayer and His Word, and allow Him to impart to you the order of your day. The psalmist also says, "Early will I seek You" (Ps. 63:1). God will teach us how to structure our days and capitalize on the time we have. How? He says to call to Him, and He will answer and show us great and mighty things we do not know. (See Jeremiah 33:3.) He orders the steps of His chosen ones (Ps. 37:23). According to Psalm 139:16, "Your eyes have seen my unformed substance; and in Your book were all written the days that were appointed for me, when as yet there was not one of them [even taking shape]" (AMP).

God has such interest in our lives that He created us and planned every day of our lives. He loves His creation so much that He is involved and interested in the details of everything that concerns us. He even knows the number of hairs on our heads.

We want to get to a place where we enjoy every moment of our day and commit every second to the Lord. It is important that we remain conscious of our time because as I've said, time is the measurement of life. How we spend our time determines the quality of our lives. By His Spirit, God will teach us how to move throughout our day and capitalize on every moment and opportunity to be in line with His perfect plan for our lives. For some of us He may even accelerate our days and times so that what was lost by the hand of the enemy is made up for and redeemed. God does not want you to be left behind. We must make our prayer, "God, teach me to number my days, that I may gain a heart of wisdom."

Here are ways to capitalize on your time.

1. Ask God for the hand of the diligent.

The chosen are not sluggards, and neither are they slothful. The chosen have the hand of the diligent.

> He who has a slack hand becomes poor, but the hand of the diligent makes rich. He who gathers in summer is a wise son; he who sleeps in harvest is a son who causes shame.
>
> —PROVERBS 10:4–5

The chosen are diligent and wise and know the times and seasons. They know when it is time to gather and when it is time to rest. Their wisdom combined with hard work brings wealth and riches into their lives.

> The hand of the diligent will rule, but the lazy man
> will be put to forced labor.
> —PROVERBS 12:24

Diligence opens doors of leadership. The diligent lead. Their work has proved them to be trustworthy, reliable, competent, and knowledgeable. They will not always be in a position to take orders. Their diligence leads them to promotion and prominence. People will seek them for instruction, direction, and guidance. Their faithfulness will cause them to rule. To them Jesus says, "You were faithful over a few things, I will make you ruler over many things" (Matt. 25:21).

If we are going to be people who live by the timing of God, we must ask the Lord to let a spirit of diligence come upon us. We cannot be slothful like the sluggard. We need to pray, "Lord, teach me how to redeem the time."

Maybe God is talking to you about this as He did with me—how much time do we spend watching television? Some people waste their lives away watching five or six hours of television a day. When you understand that you have a purpose, you prepare yourself, and maybe television becomes less important. You begin to spend your time on developing your gift or working toward the passion and desire God placed in your heart.

Though I don't want you to get religious about TV watching, do consider the fire that godly ambition ignites inside you. You may find yourself thinking about how many hours you spend in front of the television or scrolling your Facebook timeline and how that time could be spent working on your vision and preparing yourself for the platform God has for you.

I've been asked how, with my traveling and preaching schedule, I am able to pump out all these books. Well, I have to stay home sometimes when I want to go out. Or when I go to cities to preach, I do not just go touring around the city. No. I am in a hotel room somewhere, and during the day I'm writing, writing, writing. Then in the evening I'm preaching. That is my life for a season because I know I have a set time when God will bring me into the fullness of my call.

We must allow the Lord to show us how to prioritize. What is your priority? Get to work on your vision. Don't waste your time doing things that will not profit you.

2. Keep the proper attitude.

To interrupt your timing, the enemy will use offense and rejection to cause you to waste or lose time. You want to always keep the proper attitude and maintain positivity. Don't be someone who is always worrying. Worry will cause you to take your eyes off your vision. Offense stops the momentum in your life. Rejection leads to anger, bitterness, and unforgiveness, and those things throw off the timing of God in your life. They are distractions from the enemy, so make sure you keep your heart free and pure. The Bible says, "Blessed are the pure in heart, for they shall see God" (Matt. 5:8). And the chosen must forever keep their eyes on God.

God is refining us through everyday life, and He is healing our offenses and bringing us to a place of momentum. We need to make sure we get into a place where we catch that momentum, keep moving with God, and don't stagnate. We want to live our lives forward, and the way we do this is by synchronizing our lives to the time clock of heaven. We want to be in the right place at the right time, doing the right thing with the right people.

3. Each day ask God to give you your assignment.

Your anointing will increase when your assignment is clear. What has God assigned you to do? Has He assigned you to volunteer in the children's ministry? Has He assigned you to the prayer ministry? Where has God assigned you? Has He assigned you as a Sunday school teacher?

God is very strategic. He is a God of cycles, seasons, and timing. He will put you in a place where you can be trained. Sometimes you want to go forward and be set in front of thousands of people, but you've never been trained to be on that large platform. So these are the days when you need to ask God, "What is my assignment today? What can I do today to serve Your purposes in the earth and the greater purposes for which you are preparing me?"

Ask God each day for your assignment so that every dimension of your life comes into synchronization with God's timing.

4. Do what He assigns.

Once we hear from God about what our assignment is, the next thing is to do what He has assigned. We need to apply what we have heard. If God has given you an instruction and you have not done it, you will miss God's timing. Obedience to God's instruction is key to being at the appointed time and place. How many people have received the same prophecy over and over and not done anything with it? What is their life's witness? Are they moving forward? Do they complain about feeling stuck?

When you obey God, you put yourself in His timing. You remain in His timing by continuing to obey Him. If you ever feel off timing, ask God to remind you of the last thing He told you. Then do that thing. He will then move you forward to the new thing. Though some of the things God asks us to do are harder than others, the process is simple. Seek Him for your assignment, listen to what He says, and do it. Stop wasting time. Get in the cycle of God through obedience, and you will begin to understand the seasons in your life.

In my book *The Deborah Anointing*, I talk about the seasons of God. We have seasons in our lives just as the earth has natural seasons—winter, spring, summer, and fall. You can ask the Lord what season you are in. Are you in springtime? Fall? I want you to get this book and the corresponding study guide so you can learn the principles of timing.

Understanding the season of life you are in is important because when you get a prophetic word, you will have a sense for when the word will manifest. You will be able to discern if the word you received is a "right now" word or one that will come to pass in the fullness of time, in due season, sometime later, in the future. There is something called preparation. There is something called obedience. Not every word you hear will be for the present time. As we pray, God will synchronize our lives with the time clock of heaven and we will know the things on God's agenda and timetable.

God has appointments for you, and if you don't get into

His rhythm, you can miss the timing of God. We need to learn good time management. We need to learn how to manage our lives. One of my major prayers is, "Lord, help me to do what You have called me to do. I want to use my time to glorify You."

THERE IS A TIME TO MINISTER AND A TIME TO PUT FAMILY FIRST

The chosen love God. They love His presence. They love the house of God and would spend their time serving and inquiring at His temple every hour of every day if they could, but that is not the sum of their lives. The chosen are called to prioritize the aspects of their lives according to the season God has placed them in. Do you know it glorifies God for a husband and wife to spend time together? It glorifies God for you to spend time with your children.

I tell my spiritual children who are parents that, even though we are all apostolic and prophetic and love God and have assignments, there's a set time for us to raise our kids. It is not God's plan for us to sacrifice our children on the altar of ministry. Our children are only with us for eighteen years, and that time goes by quickly, so we should use that time to make them our first priority. When our kids grow up and begin lives of their own, God will open the door for us to make ministry and kingdom service our priority.

My testimony is this: I kept my daughter, Eboni, by my side when she was a child—on my hip while I preached and in the prayer closet with me as I prayed. She was my priority, and even as I served, I did the things I needed to do to prepare her. Then, next thing you know, as soon as she went away to college, doors swung wide open to the world. I was traveling every weekend and haven't stopped since. If you are a parent reading this book now, know that as you take the time to prepare your children to live good and godly lives in this season, God will open up doors for you in the next season. There is a time and season for everything under the sun.

So many seemingly godly things can get us off timing, but then there are the things of God, such as family, that we can sometimes perceive as a distraction. That is why we must pray to know the times and seasons of our lives, so that we are in synch with God's timetable. We don't want to be behind or ahead of God. To fulfill our destinies, we must be in the right place at the right time. So let us pray that God would make us into men and women of timing, that we might understand that He has a time and season for everything.

BREAKING THE SPIRIT OF DELAY

The Lord says He is breaking the spirit of delay and releasing strategies even in our dreams to position us to accelerate forward. If any place in our lives is not aligned with God's timetable, He is releasing an anointing to break all spirits of delay off our lives. When we remain connected to Him, following closely on the path and inclining our ears to His voice, He honors us by accelerating our steps at the right time to get us to where we should be.

Any attempts by the enemy to slow your progress will be reversed and your lost time will be redeemed. The Lord is saying that the devil may have tried to attack you, but he cannot stop you when God's hand is on your life. The only person who can stop you from fulfilling your destiny is you. This is why it is so important that you do what David did: strengthen yourself in the Lord and build yourself up in your most holy faith. Be ready to hear when God is setting you up for an acceleration of time.

We are in a season when God is moving us forward. He is releasing an east wind, which was the wind God used to open the Red Sea (Exod. 14:21), and God is saying that the east wind is blowing. The seas of strife set up to delay your progress and get you off timing are being blown back so that you may pass on dry and stable ground.

Take these decrees and speak them over your life. Wherever you have experienced delays and stops, God is going to break their power over your fulfilling His plan for your life according to His time.

I break the spirit and assignment of delay that has come against my life right now, in the name of Jesus. Lord, I want to do everything You have assigned to my life. Father, let the spirit of wisdom and revelation be released in my life.

Lord, I decree that I walk in total synchronization with the time clock of heaven. I loose myself from time delay spirits.

God, I decree an acceleration in my life. I will no longer lag behind time, nor will I get ahead of You.

Lord, I decree that I will be in the right place at the right time with the right people doing the right thing. I will make the right connections, and I cancel the assignment of every person assigned against my life to get me off Your path for my life.

God, remove everything and everyone—every person and every relationship—assigned to sabotage Your timing. Remove everything sent to keep me going around the mountain. I decree that I will not be like the children of Israel, walking around and around in the wilderness. Instead, I will be one who will go in and possess my goods and the land You have promised me.

Father, I decree right now that divine alignment be my portion as I accept Your assignment for my life.

Just as Esther stepped into her set time, Father, I decree that I am stepping into my set time of favor. Let the set time of favor come. Father, let me find favor. Let Your set timing be released.

I decree that I will not squander time. The precious gift You have given to us is Your timing. I will not waste Your gift of time. I will maximize every moment for Your purposes.

Lord, I give You permission to remove anything that would hinder Your purposes in my life. Remove those people or things that would hinder my life. Let me be attracted to people who will propel me into Your purposes. Send me instructors and mentors who have words of wisdom and instruction in due seasons of my life. Amen.

As I meditated on these decrees, the Lord said to me, "Michelle, tell My people that the season of acceleration I will bring them into is not about them chasing their dreams or even being awake until they're called. It's not about having great success. The ultimate goal of life is to glorify Me."

Bringing glory to God is the heart of the chosen. We will be a people that glorifies God even in our timing. When you live your life to glorify God, everything gets into alignment. God honors a person who is after His heart. Just as God said that David was a man after His own heart, I am decreeing right now that you would be after God's heart. I decree that everything you do is in alignment for your assignment.

Chapter 4

CHOSEN TO WALK
BY THE SPIRIT

If we live in the Spirit, let us also walk in the Spirit.
—GALATIANS 5:25

D O YOU REALIZE we can know the truth about our future? God says, "For I know the plans I have for you...plans to prosper you and not to harm you, plans to give you hope and a future" (Jer. 29:11, NIV). We can know these plans by tuning in to the Spirit of God.

We have talked about what it means to be chosen and live in the realm where the natural meets the supernatural. We've talked about how to get on the right path to walk in our chosen purpose and destiny. We've even discussed how to align with our chosen timetable to be right where God wants us to be at His appointed time. Now we're going to see that we must walk according to the Spirit of God for all these things to be added to us.

As I mentioned, God, being omnipresent, can be in our

future and our present at the same time, bringing us the revelation we need to flourish in our present assignment. Well, we can follow His pattern for this by tapping into the Spirit of God to hear from Him the things that concern us about our future. That is amazing, isn't it?

The devil wants to make us think that our future isn't so bright and that there is no hope in the Lord, but God is saying the opposite. He is saying the best is yet to come. He is saying that as a chosen one you have an awesome future because you dwell in the presence of God, and in His presence is fullness of joy forevermore.

So tell me, whose report will you believe?

To hear what God is saying and doing in this hour, we must be tuned in to His Spirit. We have to walk by His Spirit. Sometimes we limit ourselves in this area. We approach our lives in God from the belief that we are natural beings trying to access the spiritual. The truth is we are spiritual beings having a natural experience. We can exist in the supernatural or spiritual realm just as easily as we exist in the natural realm. Unfortunately our perspective has been skewed as a result of the curse. But we have been redeemed, and God is working to bring us to full restoration so that we can live out our supernatural destinies.

Whenever I face up to the reality that I am first supernatural, I see again how important it is for me to keep my affections on things above.

> Set your affection on things above, not on things on
> the earth.
>
> —COLOSSIANS 3:2, KJV

Affection in Colossians 3:2 is synonymous with mind, interests, affairs, feelings, thoughts, perspective, and views.[1] The things above are the heavenly things, the godly or righteous things. *Above* is the place where our minds are not in the gutter or heavy-laden with the cares of the world. The things above are "whatever things are true, whatever things are noble, whatever things are just, whatever things are pure, whatever things are lovely, whatever things are of good report," whatever things are virtuous and praiseworthy (Phil. 4:8).

This place in the Spirit is where we have the right mindset to receive the strategies God will teach us on how to press in to our future. He wants to awaken us to our destiny, and not only awaken us but also propel us there with great force.

Spirit to Spirit

First Corinthians 2:14 says, "But the natural man does not receive the things of the Spirit of God, for they are foolishness to him; nor can he know them, because they are spiritually discerned." It is important for the chosen to walk by the Spirit so we can discern what He is saying to us.

Our flesh will keep us from walking in the Spirit because it naturally opposes God and His will for our lives. We cannot walk according to our flesh and its desires and walk in the Spirit at the same time. Our flesh is centered on itself. Its only desire is to satisfy and preserve itself. It has no concern for the things of God. This is why we must build up our spirit man, so that our flesh will be subjected to it instead of itself. Our spirit is the part of our makeup that connects directly to the Spirit of God. A strong connection between our spirit and God's Spirit is what enables us to move forward on the path of life at the pace God has set.

Being filled with the Spirit of God is the first step to walking by the Spirit. This comes by way of a supernatural experience with God. I've heard stories of people who have been in deep prayer and intercession—alone, just them and God—and they've felt a burning sensation stir within them as the power and glory of God descended in the room. Some have said that all they could do was weep at the magnitude of the moment. Others spoke in tongues for the first time. Being filled can also happen by the laying on of hands, as the Bible shows in Acts 8:14–16. Most times it is accompanied by speaking in tongues or an unknown or heavenly language as evidence of being filled.

When we receive the infilling of the Holy Spirit, we are "endued with power from on high" (Luke 24:49). The word *endued* means "to sink into," to "put on," or to "be clothed."[2] When the Holy Spirit fills us, we "sink into" God's power. We become clothed in His power when we are filled with the Holy Spirit. Everyday troubles and trials do not affect us the same way because we have the power of God burning inside of us. The spirit man is strong, and in the places where our flesh used to control us, we now say, "Not my will but Thine be done." God is first in the life of the chosen one who is filled with the Spirit and walks by the Spirit.

BENEFITS OF WALKING BY THE SPIRIT

There are many benefits the chosen experience by walking according to the Spirit of God. They cannot imagine life outside of the Spirit. They have tried life on their own and experienced cycles of failure, lack, and defeat. Through these hardships they have learned the character of God and trust Him with their whole life. As a chosen one, here are the benefits you experience as you walk by the Spirit:

The Spirit is your guide on the path of life.

John 16:13 says, "However, when He, the Spirit of truth, has come, He will guide you into all truth; for He will not speak on His own authority, but whatever He hears He will speak; and He will tell you things to come."

The Spirit gives you strength to live righteously.

With God's Spirit leading our lives, we have power over our flesh (Gal. 3:13; 5:25), as I have already mentioned, and the lust of the flesh, the lust of the eyes, and the pride of life (1 John 2:16), which all act against God's plan for our lives.

As we are filled with the Spirit and walk with Him, God says, "I will give you a new heart and put a new spirit within you; I will take the heart of stone out of your flesh and give you a heart of flesh. I will put My Spirit within you and cause you to walk in My statutes, and you will keep My judgments and do them" (Ezek. 36:26–27).

He also helps us find a way out of temptation and circumstances that could compromise our right standing with Him (1 Cor. 10:13).

The Spirit teaches you.

Jesus said, "But the Helper, the Holy Spirit, whom the Father will send in My name, He will teach you all things, and bring to your remembrance all things that I said to you" (John 14:26). The Holy Spirit helps us understand Scripture. He gives us revelation on certain truths, principles, and realities so that we can discern the will of God and make wise decisions. He is sometimes referred to as the Spirit of truth who testifies of Jesus Christ (John 15:26). Truth illuminates dark places and error. The Holy Spirit teaches us the difference between truth and error and helps us to maintain faith in the person of Christ.

The Spirit is your prayer partner.

Romans 8:26–27 says, "For we do not know what we should pray for as we ought, but the Spirit Himself makes intercession for us with groanings which cannot be uttered. Now He who searches the hearts knows what the mind of the Spirit is, because He makes intercession for the saints according to the will of God."

The Spirit comforts you.

In the Amplified Bible, Classic Edition, the Holy Spirit is called the "Comforter (Counselor, Helper, Intercessor, Advocate, Strengthener, and Standby)."

The Spirit keeps life exciting.

You never know what doors the Holy Spirit will open for you or the reasons He led you through certain experiences until one day you are called forward to minister, serve, or lead out of those experiences. The Bible tells us about Paul (2 Cor. 12:1–5), Philip (Acts 8:26–40), John (Rev. 4:1–6), and others who were caught up by the Spirit and carried to another geographic location. I know modern-day prophets who experience this now, in dreams or visions and in physical reality. Not knowing where God will lead from one moment to the next is exciting for His chosen ones. Their lives are submitted to His will. Their hearts remain ever ready, saying "Send me, Lord, and I will go."

The Spirit gives you the anointing to function in certain gifts.

There are eighteen gifts of the Spirit named in Romans 12, 1 Corinthians 12, and Ephesians 4. These gifts are operational for those who believe "Jesus is [my] Lord" and those who are "under the power and influence of the Holy Spirit" (1 Cor. 12:3, AMPC). The Spirit gives to believers these "gifts, extraordinary powers distinguishing certain Christians, due to the power of divine grace operating in their souls by the Holy Spirit" (v. 4, AMPC).

These gifts are considered a manifestation of the Holy Spirit being active in a life and are given for the common good and profit of all (v. 7). They allow us to help one another beyond our simple human ability (v. 7, NLT). When the gifts of the Spirit are in operation, people are blessed, healed, delivered, and given revelation and clarity for their lives. Some people are saved because of witnessing the manifestation of the gifts of the Spirit.

The chosen naturally operate in the gifts. They exist in that realm where the gifts lie and are part of the arsenal of resources for living a kingdom life.

The Spirit is a helper.

As Jesus prepared His disciples for His departure back to heaven, He said, "And I will pray the Father, and He will give you another Helper, that He may abide with you forever" (John 14:16). The Spirit helps us in so many ways I've already named, but then He also helps us in our weakness.

Romans 8:25–26 says, "But if we hope for what we do not see, we wait for it with patience. Likewise the Spirit helps us in our weakness" (KJV). Though verse 26 of this passage is often connected with prayer, the Lord was showing Paul (who wrote the Book of Romans) that that is not the only thing we are to understand here. The word *likewise* is connecting us to the previous verse, which says, "But if we hope for what we do not see…"

There are times when we may pray and pray about something and not see it manifest in the time we think it should. I wrote about Hannah in another of my books. Her hope for a son was deferred. Her heart was sick. Some have said that when she went to the temple and prayed so fervently she drew the attention of the priest—who thought she was drunk—she was praying in the Spirit in an unknown tongue.

We could argue about whether the Holy Spirit was available at that time in that way, or we can see that God sent His Spirit to help her in her weakness. She was not eating. She was in bitterness of heart. She had endured merciless taunting by the other wife, who was fruitful. She had been coming to the temple and praying year after year with no manifestation. Though she knew whom to take her petitions to and may have known that having a son was God's will for her life, she still did not have what she hoped for.

However, she remained steadfast in hoping for what she did not see, and the Holy Spirit strengthened her.

Where we are weak concerning our hope and faith toward the promises of God that have yet to manifest in our lives, the Holy Spirit helps us. He restores our souls and helps us wait with patience.

> Wait on the LORD; be of good courage, and He shall strengthen your heart; wait, I say, on the LORD!
> —PSALM 27:14

The Holy Spirit is a force of supernatural power that becomes the indwelling I Am in the lives of God's people. I've shown the many ways here that we benefit from walking in the Spirit. The power of the Holy Spirit is not just for a Sunday morning shout and dance. No. He is active in our lives when we actively engage with Him, call on Him, stir up the gifts that are in us, obey His voice, follow His lead, and apply to our everyday lives His revealed truths. His power is available to us in whatever form we need to walk out the chosen and set-apart life.

PROPELLED INTO PURPOSE

Walking by the Spirit helps you to become a winner at life. As you grow in your gifts and ability to hear when the Spirit says go here or go there, say this or say that, you will see the reality of living in both the natural and supernatural realms open up to you. I'm telling you, these are the days when the Spirit of God is releasing His mysteries to His chosen ones so that we can manifest His glory in the earth. It is His desire for you to prosper and walk fully in your purpose. If you do not, you are not testifying of

His existence. He must cause you to win, He must give you power to get wealth, and He must cause His grace and blessing to overtake you.

I think of the time in 1 Samuel 30:8 when David had lost everything to a band of soldiers—his wife and children, his men's wives and children, and all their possessions. David asked the Lord, "Should I go after them?" The Lord answered him, "Pursue, for you shall surely overtake them and without fail recover all." He was saying, "Yes, David, go. You will win the fight and take back everything that was taken from you."

Maybe you are in a season when you are looking at the devastation of everything that has been taken. Maybe your home situation, finances, or personal foundation feels as if it has been set ablaze by the enemy. Here's what I want you to understand about your future: you win. As you walk by the Spirit, the Spirit guarantees that though the thief may come to steal, kill, and destroy, and he may launch attacks or fiery darts, neither his tactics nor his weapons will prosper. You are chosen. You will "surely overtake them and without fail recover all."

Whatever negative things the devil is saying about your future, that you will not accomplish what God set in your heart to do or that you have lost everything and there is no hope, you know that he is a liar. You understand your covenant with the Lord Jesus Christ, that it is His will for you to prosper and be in good health even as your soul prospers. So what you are dealing with is not reality; it's your feelings. The devil loves to attack us with feelings of failure, feelings that we're not going to make it.

Some of you reading this book now are at a certain place in your life, and maybe there are things you thought should have happened by now, but they have not. God is going to cause an anointing to come over you, and you will receive the power and grace to overtake your enemies and apprehend those things that God has ordained for you. That word *overtake* means to move forward with a great force. I believe the spirit of pursuit that stirs inside you will come with a spiritual force behind it that makes you unstoppable. This supernatural grace will propel us into our futures, but we have to pursue what He said we would recover. That word *pursue* means to go after with great intensity.

When God told David to pursue and then overtake, that word *overtake* means "to reach," "to take hold upon," "attain to," "to be able to secure."[3] In my mind, I also see it as meaning to be prepared ahead of; to run alongside, but to propel ahead of. I believe God is releasing great acceleration into our lives. We discussed this in the previous chapter. Whatever God has assigned you to do, you are going to be the best in it because you walk by His Spirit.

God said, "Pursue, for you shall surely overtake them and without fail recover all." Do you know that is a promise from God? It is an oath. God is saying, "Don't be afraid about your future. Don't be afraid about what I'm putting in your heart, for you are going to do it. You will pursue, overtake, and recover all."

God promises that this will be your future. You are a winner. You are victorious. You have what it takes to enter the battle and recover all the spoils. God wants to bless you in this way. For this is His whole purpose. He designed you to be fruitful, to multiply, and to subdue the earth. God wants you to take dominion. But you cannot have dominion without prosperity. So God is saying in this hour, "Whatever the enemy has tried to take from you, I am going to release a spiritual force that will propel you into a future where you recover it all."

The truth about your future is that it is good. I don't care what the spirit of despair and rejection is trying to show you. God said, "Tell my people that the truth about their future is that I am blessing them." Selah.

LEAN IN TO THE SPIRIT AND MANIFEST THE IMPOSSIBLE

Throughout the Scriptures we see examples of how God demonstrated His power when people walked in obedience to His Spirit. In the Book of Exodus, God delivered the children of Israel from Egyptian slavery. With Moses leading them, they had seen signs and wonders and had God's protection over them. But in Exodus 14 we find that they reached a dead stop and had nowhere farther to run, with the Red Sea in front of them and Pharaoh's army behind them. The people were very afraid and complained to Moses, "Because there were no graves in Egypt, have you taken us away to die in the wilderness? Why have you so dealt with us, to bring us up out of Egypt? Is this not the word that we told you in Egypt, saying, 'Let us alone that we may serve the Egyptians'? For it would have been better for us to serve the Egyptians than that we should die in the wilderness" (vv. 11–12).

Moses encouraged them and with the faith of a chosen one said, "Do not be afraid. Stand still, and see the salvation of the LORD, which He will accomplish for you today. For the Egyptians whom you see today, you shall see again no more forever. The LORD will fight for you, and you shall hold your peace" (vv. 13–14).

In reality there was nothing Moses could do in and of himself. They were facing sudden death. This situation was impossible. Knowing his limitations, yet having experienced God's unlimited power throughout their exodus, Moses went to God, and He said, "Tell the children of Israel to go forward. But lift up your rod, and stretch out your hand over the sea and divide it. And the children of Israel shall go on dry ground through the midst of the sea" (Exod. 14:15–16). And it was so—the impossible became possible by the enduing of Holy Spirit power upon Moses.

Sometimes it may look as if you can't walk through something or accomplish it. In the natural realm there's nothing you can do except pull on God. These things require you to lean in to the Spirit of God. The rod in Moses' example represents your mouth. You have to stretch out your rod. You must open your mouth and declare what you know God has told you to do.

By His Spirit, God dropped the prophet Ezekiel into an impossible scenario. Ezekiel 37 recounts it for us.

> The hand of the LORD came upon me and brought
> me out in the Spirit of the LORD, and set me down
> in the midst of the valley; and it was full of bones.
> Then He caused me to pass by them all around, and
> behold, there were very many in the open valley;
> and indeed they were very dry.
> —EZEKIEL 37:1–2

Then verses 4–5 say:

> Again He said to me, "Prophesy to these bones
> and say to them, 'O dry bones, hear the word of
> the LORD! Thus says the Lord GOD to these bones:
> "Surely I will cause breath to enter into you, and you
> shall live."'"

Yes, God told him to prophesy. Now, some of you may say, "Prophetess, I'm not a prophet." And, of course, all of God's chosen are not called to the fivefold ministry office of prophet. But we still need to be prophetic. We still need to learn how the prophetic realm is a spiritual gift that God has given for anyone who is filled with the Holy Spirit. Anyone who is part of the redemptive plan of God ought to be able to hear God speak to him or her and say and do what He says. It was what Jesus paid for on the cross. The prophetic is one of our spiritual weapons.

If you are reading this book, you have already engaged with the prophetic. You may have received several prophetic words about your purpose. You need to speak them over yourself. You need to get the promise of God for your life and begin to prophesy. God's purposes will begin to happen, and things will come together when you begin to speak them. I don't care what it looks like in the natural. You have to speak what God has said over you. You have to declare the Word of God. Some people who are prophetic and apostolic just prophesy by rote. They've become too familiar with the prophetic. But I'm telling you, there is a coming unction where God is calling us to lift up our voices and prophesy, to decree a thing so that it will be established (Job 22:28).

The truth about your future is in your mouth. You have to create it. You have to speak it. You have to declare it.

When Ezekiel obeyed and declared the word of the Lord, he began to see movement. When you start declaring things, movement begins to happen in the spirit first before it happens in the natural. This is why walking by the Spirit is important to the chosen, because you cannot walk by sight. You must walk by faith. You cannot get distracted by what is going on around you and then try to speak. Look into your situation with eyes of faith so that instead of cursing it, you prophesy to it. Don't curse your crisis. Don't curse your despair. Begin to speak what God has said. Declare His Word.

That's part of being a believer. That's the privilege: we are made in the image of God, and we have to say what God is telling us to say. Take the prophetic words you've received out, if you've kept them written down somewhere, and begin to declare them. If you believe the prophetic word is true, speak it over the dry areas of your life, and indeed you will look and see sinews and flesh come upon those bones; skin will cover them, and they will breathe, come alive, and stand on their feet (Ezek. 37:7–8).

RISE UP AND PROSPER BY THE SPIRIT OF GOD

Ezekiel 37 goes on to say:

> Therefore prophesy and say to them, "Thus says the Lord GOD: 'Behold, O My people, I will open your graves and cause you to come up from your graves, and bring you into the land of Israel. Then you shall know that I am the LORD, when I have opened your graves, O My people, and brought you up from your graves. I will put My Spirit in you, and you shall

live, and I will place you in your own land. Then
you shall know that I, the LORD, have spoken it and
performed it,' says the LORD."

—EZEKIEL 37:12–14

I believe God is speaking this word over us today. God is
saying that He will place us in our own land. Land refers
to the place we've been given to take dominion. He prepares us for this by first putting His Spirit in us. Then He
will open the graves. By opening the graves for us in the
Spirit, God is saying that He will open whatever part of
our lives or spirits have been locked and bound.

Maybe you have bound and blocked emotions to the
point that you don't know how to love. You are waiting
on your husband. You are waiting for friendship, but the
real reason those relationships have yet to flourish is you
are the one who needs God to open up the graves of your
emotions. By His Spirit, He will loose you from those
graveclothes. You will be free to love, free to laugh, free to
prosper, and free to enjoy life.

Seize this moment! Don't let the devil take any more
from you. Make a decision to walk in joy, to delight yourself in the Lord, so that He will give you the desires of
your heart. No matter what the devil says through isolation, no matter what he tries to tell you through the rejection, your future is bright. Your relationships will flourish.
Your dreams will manifest. God wants you to know that
He has a future and a hope for you.

Get ready to be shifted to a new level of joy in your own
land that God is giving you. Acts 17:26–28 says that God
has determined our preappointed times and the boundaries of our dwelling. God knows where you should live.

He knows how much land you should have. He knows where you should set up your business or nonprofit. He knows the geographic areas He is assigning you to, and by His Spirit, He will cause you to prophesy His word over those areas so they will come to fruition.

Everybody has a land. Everybody has a set boundary. God has set them. Yours may be ten, fifteen, or two acres. Whatever your measure of rule is, God says, "I'm going to set you in your own land that you may rule." We all have a place where we can prosper. There is a place of dominion for each one of us. We cannot allow the devil to keep us in a small place when God has a wealthy place for us. The truth about your future is that God is taking you through to your wealthy place.

You may feel as though you have been through so many trials and tests, and as a result you have lost so much. But I'm telling you to rise up as a chosen one in this hour and begin to move with the Spirit of God. The Lord has told me over and over again throughout the years that He is breaking the spirit of poverty and poverty mindset off the body of Christ. The ultimate purpose of poverty is to stop you from doing the will of God, but the Lord said He is releasing His Spirit of wisdom and power to gain financial independence.

With financial independence you can obey God to the fullest. If God tells you to build a church or revitalize a community, you will have the financial independence to obey Him. God is releasing an unprecedented amount of wealth and riches to the body of Christ. Real financial independence is when you can do what God has designed you to do with no economic restrictions. This is what I mean when I speak about a spiritual force. Prosperity in the hands of the chosen is a force.

We are being propelled and thrusted into a bright future. We are going to excel head and shoulders above the rest. We are going to overtake every assignment and accomplish the work we have been sent to do, not by might nor by power, but by the Spirit of God.

God is going to restore to us everything "the locust hath eaten, the cankerworm, and the caterpiller, and the palmerworm" (Joel 2:25, KJV). But just like David, you have to rise up by the Spirit of God and go after what is yours. What you recover will be so much that you will have to give it away.

One of the greatest tests God takes us through before He releases wealth and riches is to break selfishness. Those who have a selfish spirit and think only of "me, myself, and I" will only have a certain measure, perhaps just enough to cover their immediate needs. They will not be blessed with excess. The chosen, however, are known for their kindness and generosity. This is the hour when God is opening up new things—buildings, property, opportunity, promotion, and equipment—for His chosen people who have visions to make His name famous and a heart to bring in the harvest and restore human life. You must catch that vision.

Chapter 5

SOZO: UNLOCKING THE
FULLNESS OF GOD'S
PLAN FOR YOUR LIFE

*Then God blessed them, and God said to them, "Be
fruitful and multiply; fill the earth and subdue it; have
dominion over the fish of the sea, over the birds of the
air, and over every living thing that moves on the earth."*
—GENESIS 1:28

W E COME INTO the kingdom of God through
His saving us from the effects of sin, which
without salvation would lead to eternal death
(Rom. 6:23). We receive this free gift as a result of our
confessed faith in Jesus and acceptance of His death on
the cross (Eph. 2:8–9). He took the effects of sin on Himself so that we would not have to (Rom. 3:21–31). With
salvation comes full restoration to the dominion and
authority we had before the fall of Adam and Eve in the

Garden of Eden (Luke 10:19). Jesus rescued, redeemed, and restored us to favor with God. When we accept our salvation, we become new creations (2 Cor. 5:17). We exchange our old lives of sin and self-destruction—ones that were open to torment from the enemy—and take on new lives of righteousness, blessing, and eternal purpose.

God's plan for our creation is restored through salvation. The fellowship and intimacy God desired to have with us can happen again when our sins are washed away. God's glory and sin cannot coexist. It is one or the other with God—He would rather us be hot or cold. Because of the cross Jesus' blood now covers our sinfulness so that we can boldly come into the presence of God and receive the full benefits of being His children.

We "are a chosen generation, a royal priesthood, a holy nation, His own special people, that you may proclaim the praises of Him who called you out of darkness into His marvelous light; who once were not a people but are now the people of God, who had not obtained mercy but now have obtained mercy" (1 Pet. 2:9–10).

God gave His Son to restore us to a favored and chosen position with God. We get the full advantage by choosing Him in return by receiving the gift of salvation. As I mentioned before, many are called, but few are chosen. We arrive at chosen status by choosing to live a lifestyle of holiness, one that reflects the character of God in every sphere of life, community, government, and culture. The chosen choose to walk the narrow path that makes them worthy of being God's glory carriers in the earth. Upon accepting the call to a chosen lifestyle, the chosen also recommit to carrying out the Genesis 1:28 mandate. They commit to taking full dominion and authority in whatever realm God assigns, and they will expand in that area and be fruitful in every way.

When we receive salvation, we receive the full measure of God's plan to restore us to our pre-fall status. In Greek the word for *salvation* is *sōtēria*, which means "deliverance, preservation, safety, salvation" and "deliverance from the molestation of enemies."[1] It is derived from the root word *sozo*, which means "to save, i.e. deliver or protect (literally or figuratively):—heal, preserve, save (self), do well, be (make) whole."[2] *Sozo* is used 110 times in the New Testament in verses such as Matthew 1:21, which says (emphasis added):

> And she will bring forth a Son, and you shall call His name JESUS, for He will *save* His people from their sins.

And in Matthew 9:22, in reference to complete healing (emphasis added):

> But Jesus turned around, and when He saw her He said, "Be of good cheer, daughter; your faith has made you *well*." And the woman was made *well* from that hour.

And, referring back to salvation, in John 3:17 (emphasis added):

> For God did not send His Son into the world to condemn the world, but that the world through Him might be *saved*.

Both words are used in Acts 4:12:

> Nor is there salvation in any other, for there is no other name under heaven given among men by which we must be saved.

These two Greek words show that salvation is not just about getting to heaven. Salvation is for the saving, deliverance, and restoration of the whole person in this life *and* in the life to come. Salvation includes the prosperity, fullness, and blessing of God in every aspect of your life—family, finances, business, ministry, marriage, health, and your eternity. God wants to expand the boundaries of your dwelling just as He intended to before Adam and Eve fell into temptation. He desires to enlarge your territory, and He has a plan to do it.

Through God's plan of salvation, everything the enemy set against God's people is reversed and restored through the blood of Jesus. It has always been in the heart and mind of God to command His blessing toward His chosen ones.

Blessing and expansion were the first things He spoke to His new creation: "Be fruitful and multiply; fill the earth and subdue it; have dominion over the fish of the sea, over the birds of the air, and over every living thing that moves on the earth" (Gen. 1:28). This verse provides the four-point foundation for living out a chosen destiny:

1. Be fruitful.

2. Multiply.

3. Fill the earth.

4. Take dominion.

Sometimes it is hard to believe or receive that God only wants the very best for His chosen ones. Sometimes, because of life's hardship, we believe that God is angry at us, and to appease Him, we have to jump through hoops and do all kinds of religious rituals to gain His favor. But from creation it has always been God's heart to bless us and make our lives full and prosperous in every way.

THE CHOSEN FAMILY

Marriage is the first institution established by God. He took a good man and a good woman and put them together. Millennia since, He is still doing the same thing. If you are married, know that God has a chosen purpose for your marriage. With God you and your spouse are the epitome of a power couple. Though you each have special and individual assignments, there is something God has called you to do together—something that you cannot do separately. However, both people must have a yes in their heart.

If you are single, desiring a mate, God has a special plan and purpose for you even while you wait. Some of the most powerful moments in life occur in the stage between the dream and the fulfillment. Do not despise your winter season. I encourage you to get my book *The Hannah Anointing* to learn how to handle seasons of delay.

When it comes to raising your children in the fullness of God, realize that nothing sneaks up on God and nothing sneaks up on you, because you are chosen, and they are too. Sometimes we are so hungry for God and focused on pleasing Him that we put raising our children second to the call of God on our lives. As I said earlier, don't feel as if you are missing the call of God by spending time pouring into your children.

God has a prosperity plan for your whole family. He has designed you to rule and reign together. When God is the center, no one will feel as if other family members are a distraction but that you all are placed strategically together for God's glory to be displayed through your unity and cohabitation.

BE FRUITFUL FIRST, THEN MULTIPLY

God wants us to be fruitful, and with His power we need to come against all the things in our lives that stop fruitfulness. We must be fruitful before we can multiply. The key to fruitfulness is tapping into the vine that is Jesus Christ. In John 15:5 Jesus said, "I am the vine, you are the branches. He who abides in Me, and I in him, bears much fruit; for without Me you can do nothing."

Once you have fruit, you can begin to multiply. We cannot be fruitful if we do not abide or remain in Christ. Some of the defining characteristics of the chosen are holiness, faith, and obedience. When we are not doing what it takes to walk according to the Spirit and having a walk worthy of the Lord, which we will discuss in a later chapter, we will not stay intimately connected to Christ. The Bible says that the branches of those who do not remain in Christ wither and they are cast out and thrown into the fire. God gets glory when you are fruitful, so we shouldn't get trapped in the belief that God is pleased when we are trying to live and prosper with meager resources and meager incomes.

God is glorified when you prosper in spirit and by the

work of your hands. He is the One who empowers us to get wealth. He gave up His riches in heaven and became poor so that we might become rich (2 Cor. 8:9). He came to redeem us in every way and to restore us to His full image—spiritually, emotionally, physically, and economically. We cannot be a blessing when we are not blessed.

God is preparing His chosen ones for the greatest wealth transfer we've ever known. He knows that we need the wisdom and revelation to steward it according to His plan. This is where He takes us through a process of building the right character and integrity to manage the fruit. If we are selfish and filled with the lust of the flesh and the lust of the eyes, if we have vain ambition, the increase will go right past us into the hands of those whose hearts are after His. God can only work with submitted vessels and contrite hearts.

The chosen must find all sufficiency in God, Jehovah Jireh, and know that He alone is more than enough before they can be trusted with the overflow. When He sees that we can handle the fruit and have the capacity to manage more, we will begin to see the fruit multiply and fill the earth. So it is then through this prosperity that we multiply and give and are generous. When we believe and obey God in the area of our finances, we show it through our tithes and offerings.

Multiplication then becomes about influence. We cannot be influential on the earth without fruit and without weight. As we grow, increase, and expand, then the boundaries of our dwelling, our territory, and our measure of rule are enlarged. We take on a Jabez-like anointing (1 Chron. 4:9–10). But you will be expanded only into territories that God has specifically assigned you.

He knows the territory you can handle and will reveal it to you as you remain in Him, inquiring, listening, and obeying. Our expansion and taking dominion over our enemies is part of our reclaiming what was already ours before the fall and part of God's full plan of salvation.

REDEMPTION, PURSUIT, AND RECOVERY

Sin takes us far away from God and His plan for our lives, but God's plan to free us from sin helps us find our way back to the path of life and get back into position to recover what sin has taken from us. First Samuel 30 is a powerful chapter regarding recovering the blessings of God. In this chapter we find David, God's man, under deadly attack. He had been fleeing from Saul, who was supposed to be his mentor. Taken somewhat off guard by the betrayal, not only did David not want to fight Saul, but he also did not know how to. Sometimes when we don't know how to fight a particular enemy, we tend to get in the flesh. This is exactly how David responded. He went and fought with his enemies without God leading him, and if we put it in our terms, he ended up in a backslidden state. That is where we find him in 1 Samuel 30. Read 1 Samuel 27 up to 30 to get the context of what I'm sharing.

Ultimately David did not want to fight Saul, but Saul, possessed by jealousy and a spirit of competition, was after him. These are the spirits that are also at work in our lives to kill our destinies. Even though salvation has been granted, we are still in a spiritual warfare to secure what God has for us, so we have to learn how to defend against certain enemies. Let's see now how David, having stepped out of the will of God, was able to repent and get back into right standing to pursue the enemy and recover all that had been stolen.

First Samuel 30:1–2 says, "Now it happened, when David and his men came to Ziklag, on the third day, that the Amalekites had invaded the South and Ziklag, attacked Ziklag and burned it with fire, and had taken captive the women and those who were there, from small to great; they did not kill anyone, but carried them away and went their way." Notice that the text says, "Now it happened…" Something did indeed happen: David was out of his place. He was fighting with the enemies of God. He had aligned himself with the Philistines. (See 1 Samuel 27.)

The ambush took place while David was out of his position, while he was not at home. Think about it. When we're not in our position, somebody is suffering. This is important because we need to understand just how significant we are to the people around us, to the people to whom we are assigned. Everybody is called to do something that contributes to the body, group, family, team, or community he or she has been placed in. So while David was missing in action from the place he was assigned to, the enemy came in and attacked his wife and children.

Whenever you are not doing what God designed you to do, you are opening the door for the enemy to attack those you are responsible for. Adam and Eve did this as they walked through the garden one day—Eve ended up in a conversation with the devil at the forbidden tree, and Adam, well, there is no account of his whereabouts. What we do know is that when God came looking for them at their usual place in the cool of the day, they were not there. (See Genesis 3.) From one scene to the next we see that they were not in the places that God called them to be in.

Their actions left all of mankind vulnerable to the temptation and torment of the enemy. As the first parents, they were responsible for all the future generations that would come from their seed.

Since then we have been in a fight with the enemy of our souls to maintain our position—first restoring our ability to stand before God through redemption, then hearing God to learn what our position is, then using our spiritual weapons to defend against the enemy, who tries to get us out of position day in and day out.

But we cannot give up our position, and it can be so hard sometimes. Even I have been guilty of wanting to move from my position in the prophetic, seeing so many people merchandising the prophetic realm. It can get so bad that I will just say, "I'm not going to be a part of it anymore."

But then God says, "Yeah. While you are somewhere sulking or somewhere distracted doing something else, you are not on your post as a watchman, as a mother in the realm of the prophetic, as one who is called to lead and help people understand that dimension."

Listen, we cannot relent. We must come to a place where if we have moved out of position, we begin to quickly recover it. There's too much at stake. Whenever you are out of alignment with the will of God, God still will extend grace to you to recover. But you can't do it in the flesh. You must inquire of the Lord.

1. Ask God to teach you how to enter into the fullness of His plan for your life.

There's always something going on in the spirit. God tells us, "My ways are not like yours. My thoughts are not like yours." (See Isaiah 55:8–9.) They are so much higher, but we can ask God to help us know His plans and how He is working things out for our good. Sometimes we can't see things because the mundane routine attacks that come from the enemy distract us. So we can ask God to help us shift back into the right mindset.

God is cultivating in us the hearts of warriors and leaders, just as He did with David. David was called to be king, but he was acting as if he didn't know God. So the first thing he had to do was strengthen himself in the Lord (1 Sam. 30:6). At his weakest, most distressed point, David aligned himself with the Philistines. He was so tired of fighting Saul (fighting the system) and trying to walk in righteousness that the enemy attacked his heart. Your greatest weapon is always your heart. You have to keep your heart pure, and you can only do that by strengthening yourself in the Lord, inquiring of the Lord, and getting His strategies.

2. Understand that God will bring you into your land to possess it.

David was in the wrong place fighting with the wrong people, and while he was there, the enemy came in and took his family. We need to make sure we ask God, "What is my territory? Where are my boundaries?" He will bring you into your territory and show you the boundaries of your dwelling (Acts 17:26). Each of us has a specific territory we are supposed to occupy.

In coming into the land God has for us, we must also submit to God's plan for us to prosper there. Many times we fail or make bad decisions because we are not in the right place. Just because you have knowledge of certain

103

things does not mean that is your primary place or assignment. We don't have strength to be everywhere and do everything. And we want to be careful of being pulled into ministries or projects at work that are not in line with what we are assigned to. Sometimes we get into people pleasing, and because it may seem to give us favor with a person for a moment, we get out of place trying to do what makes them happy. Beloved, we don't want to go into this place where we put pleasing people above pleasing God.

Once you have asked God to show you your territory, you need to dwell there. God knows where we are supposed to be, and when you understand the boundary of your dwelling, you can take dominion.

EVERYBODY HAS A GARDEN

When God set Adam and Eve in the garden, He blessed them and said, "Be fruitful and multiply." Many of us may not be fruitful because we don't understand the blessing that is already on our lives. As a believer, as one who loves the Lord, and as one who is saved, understand that God has blessed you. Fruitfulness flows out of your renewed mindset of being blessed by God. The devil will often try to attack your faith, and your unbelief will lead you to behave as if God is not on your side, as if He doesn't love you, as if His heart isn't to see you grow and prosper. You will begin to sin through cycles of failure and defeat.

But God's full plan of redemption is to break the demonic mindset that set you up to fail—spirits of rejection, unworthiness, and even poverty. He is breaking barrenness in this hour. His Spirit is reaching out to those who desire to know the reality and fullness of His salvation.

Reaching out to Him in return and asking Him, "Where is your place of fruitfulness?" is one of the first major things we need to do to be reset, refocused, and redeemed in this area. Everyone has a garden—a place where we can flourish, grow, and multiply.

With the leading of the Holy Spirit, examine your life and who you are. Examine your strengths and your failures. Look back at the words that have been spoken to you through prophecy and prayer.

You are going to go from a place of dreaming to a place of activating dreams through the divine strategies God will give. God set Adam and Eve in the Garden of Eden. That was their place of dominion, but they didn't know how to care for it or how to make it grow and flourish. God taught them. He taught them how to care for everything over which He gave them authority. He will do the same for you.

Plans Change; Purpose Doesn't

Your plan for success can change, but your purpose will never change. Though the enemy sets up thorns and traps and devices to come against God's plan, God still has a way. He has a purpose for your life, though sometimes the plan to fulfill it is contingent upon your actions and the actions of other people. It was not God's plan for Adam and Eve to sin, but His ultimate purpose for creating man was not thwarted. He made a way through Jesus to restore our connection with Him. There are circumstances where the enemy ravages us or the things for which we are responsible. Relationships are damaged. Trusts are broken. Business ventures fail. You may have inquired of the Lord and heard His purpose for your life, but because of actions that occurred in the natural as a result of free will, a certain plan to fulfill it in that way didn't work. Don't be stubborn. Let it go. If it's not fruitful, let it go. As you do, God can give you another plan. He does not want you to stay in a place where you are being abused or where people are attacking you.

This is just one of the many things that gets me so excited about serving the Lord Jesus Christ. He is the God of redemption. He redeems our lives from destruction. He always makes a way if we repent. If you make mistakes, if something devastating has happened to you, God always can provide a new way of escape. We have to be flexible. Our trust in His overall purpose can free us from being so rigid. For instance, at one time you might have thought, "I know what God told me. God told me to go to this place. God told me to go to this church." While at one time God might have wanted you to be delivered at a particular church, don't let the place of your one-time deliverance become the place of your captivity. In Saul's kingdom David was delivered, trained, and equipped and learned how to fight. But suddenly Saul began to turn on him, and David had to get out of there. He had to run for his life. He never turned around and fought Saul. David had to uproot himself from the place he knew, and because of his flexibility with how God would fulfill his purpose, God did something new in his life.

I believe God wanted a smooth transition between Saul and David, but David didn't know how to fight Saul. The plan was for David to be raised up in that kingdom, but the plan changed. David's purpose, however, to be king over Israel never changed.

Beloved, we have to count it all joy when we fall under divers trials and temptations because the trying of our faith produces repentance. The trying of our faith produces patience. When patience has its perfect work on the inside of us, we build the strength to endure anything and still be fruitful.

Chapter 6

UNGODLY BELIEFS
AND MINDSETS THAT
ATTACK THE CHOSEN

*But be transformed by the renewing of your
mind, that you may prove what is that good
and acceptable and perfect will of God.*
—ROMANS 12:2

IN THE PREVIOUS chapter we discussed God's redemption plan and how it sets us back to God's original purpose and intent for creating us, as well as putting us in a position to reestablish the blessing of Genesis 1:28, which is to be fruitful and multiply. While this plan aligns us with our purpose, some things can sidetrack us and even hinder God's plan. In this chapter we will look at specific beliefs and mindsets that come against the chosen life and how we can break free from all of them and move toward our ultimate purpose in victory.

One of the first ideas we need to understand, and one that will set many of us free, is that the chosen are not perfect; they are just loved by God. They are regular, everyday people like you and me who do not come from perfect backgrounds. They are not super-saints. They are born and shaped in iniquity just like the rest of the human race. They have the propensity to be affected by generational curses, ungodly beliefs, and broken mindsets that rise up against them.

Consider the original chosen people of Israel—they were messed up and dysfunctional. The prophets, kings, and even some of the judges, such as Samson, were deeply flawed. They faced horrendous seasons of war and captivity and often found themselves desolated by the enemy. But every time, God loved them and rescued and redeemed them.

In 2 Chronicles 20 we come to a time when the people of Israel faced up against an army they knew they could not beat. Defeat seemed inevitable. "O our God," they cried out in verse 12, "will You not judge them? For we have no power against this great multitude that is coming against us; nor do we know what to do, but our eyes are upon You."

See, there is a gentle dance within the body of Christ because nobody really likes to talk about the judgments of God. But what I am hearing God say is that He is getting ready to judge your enemies. His judgments are part of His justice enacted on behalf of His people. The Bible says righteousness and justice are the foundations of His throne. To clear your land of enemy occupation, He said He is getting ready to judge them and His justice will roll like a river in your life.

Isaiah 59:17 says, "For He put on righteousness as a breastplate, and a helmet of salvation on His head; He put on the garments of vengeance for clothing, and was clad with zeal as a cloak." God says, "Vengeance is mine." Let the Lord work out your victories. Justice will be met on both sides. He will not overlook one bit of evidence, for He keeps good records.

> For God is not unjust. He will not forget how hard you have worked for him and how you have shown your love to him by caring for other believers, as you still do.
>
> —HEBREWS 6:10, NLT

As it was for the people of Israel, it is like this for us today: We must cry out for justice. We must use our war weapons in this hour as God is fighting with us. To be clear, when I say "enemies," I am speaking about demons and devils. I am not talking about people, because we do not fight against flesh and blood but against principalities and powers of darkness in high places. At the end of the day it's not about people, and it's not even about you. It's about the power of God inside of you. It's about the assignment on your life the devil is trying to stop.

I don't care how many of them are battling against you. There are more *for* you than against you. Begin to declare your day of breakthrough. Begin to declare the day of justice. Bow down and worship as the people of Israel did as they faced their enemies. Declare, "Lord, You are the God of justice. I cry out for Your justice. Let it roll in my life." You are a chosen overcomer.

As I alluded to at the beginning of this chapter, many of these beliefs and mindsets that work against our destinies are broken through the revelation of the love of

Father God. In this chapter I want to expose some of the
weapons the enemy forms against chosen ones and how to
overcome them.

THE SPIRIT OF POVERTY

God is causing us to walk into new levels of freedom,
authority, and prosperity. With some of us it will start
with His breaking off the poverty mindset. The ultimate
goal of the spirit of poverty is to stop us from doing the
will of God. Have you ever said, "If I had the money, I
would travel to the nations," "If I had the money, I would
give it to my church to build the new sanctuary," "If I
had the money..."? These words will not remain in our
vocabulary.

Our financial independence is not for more stuff; financial independence is about obedience. You are supposed
to have financial independence so you can fully obey God.
He said, "I come that you may have life and have it more
abundantly." (See John 10:10.)

For a few months some time ago I was in a grumpy
mood. I had been crying out to the Lord about some
things He put on my heart to do for the kingdom. I prayed,
"Lord, I have been a faithful steward. Lord, I have blessed
so many people. Where is my fullness?" The Lord began
to show me things about myself. He said, "Michelle, you
have a poverty mindset that I need to break off of you. I
will teach you stewardship so that you can begin to move
to a place of prosperity."

God will do this for those of us who need that financial
breakthrough to begin to fund the kingdom. Now, I know
that not every believer is having issues with money, but

for those of us who do, God wants to deliver us from the spirit of poverty. The roots of this spirit go deep for some, back into generations of family that have been oppressed in this area. As I will discuss throughout the chapter, deliverance from this and other spirits will have a lot to do with our sober self-examination. We will need to be honest about areas we need deliverance from, which can first happen through prayer and prophetic ministry. But we will also need to be ready to educate ourselves about money and to implement real stewardship and discipline toward our appetites, desires, motives, and habits. Taking classes, reading books, and getting a mentor who has wealth and understands how money works are ways that we can begin to see lasting breakthroughs in our finances.

Throughout this book I am also bringing the discussion about divine wisdom and revelation concerning the witty ideas and inventions God will download to us as our ears and hearts are inclined to His voice. Some of these will bring an influx of finances and promotion as we excel in these gifts. We will become fruitful in every good work.

The Spirit of Prejudice

We've been looking back at David's experience at Ziklag, and in 1 Samuel 30:11, after David was released to pursue and overtake the enemy and recover all that had been taken from him, he met an Egyptian. This Egyptian told David the location of the band of men that had his stuff. This Egyptian man represents unconventional people—people who are not in the kingdom or in your circle or network. He represents people you may not know, someone of a different nationality perhaps. Such people may be the ones who know how to direct you to get your stuff back. They may be able to give you the skill you need. This is what I call a divine connection. If you've got a religious heart, where there may be prejudice—and people of color can be prejudiced too—you better ask God to purify your heart.

Your Egyptian could come in the form of a Caucasian, an Indian, an Asian, a rich, poor, or disabled person. You don't know who God has in place to bring forth your vision and purpose. But I believe God is going to give you eyes to see, ears to hear, and a heart to perceive what He is doing.

To be able to see who this Egyptian may be in our lives—if we have issues of prejudice in our hearts—we have to ask God to give us forgiving hearts. We cannot have the spirit of prejudice. I understand that some of us have suffered at the hands of different ethnic groups. Some who are African American, like me, have suffered at the hands of white men. We've been in slavery, but we're in the kingdom. We have the power of God to heal us and renew our minds by His Spirit. If we truly want to overcome the tragic effects of any of our painful ethnic past—Native Americans, Jews, and others—we have to let God bring healing to us and forgive.

No racial or ethnic group can stop you, not even the US president himself. When God says it is your time to prosper, when God says it is your time to do what He knitted inside of you to do, you need to be ready to be catapulted to the next level. Don't let unforgiveness stop you. When you don't forgive, it's almost as if those hurtful actions continue to inflict wounds on your life. They keep causing pain as long as you don't let them go.

This is such a season when God will show you things

that are in you. Once He knows that you are ready to walk in the fullness, that you are not going to squander it, and that He has dealt with your heart to mature it, you will start seeing breakthrough.

THE ORPHAN SPIRIT

I believe perhaps the greatest curse on the earth today is the orphan spirit. Many of us who are called to live a chosen life deal with this spirit. We may have experienced rejection from our fathers and as a result become vulnerable to various spiritual enemies, such as poverty, molestation, and abandonment. Sometimes this spirit is compounded when as a child a person is sent away from his or her biological parents to live with other relatives. As a result, that person may have never felt the love of a father or mother and was left to search out love and acceptance on his or her own.

When we accept Christ, we learn of His love and the love of the Father, which could trump the lack of love and value we experienced early in our lives. Yet this love may be hard to grasp when the most important people in our lives were not able to express love in the way we needed. So even in Christ we still struggle with father rejection, people pleasing, and fears of both failure and success. We become apprehensive of pursuing the chosen life because we are still searching for a firm foundation.

A reluctance to respond to the call to live a chosen life and then sudden compliance with God's commands to walk in power and authority against principalities that are running rampant in our culture, threatening death and destruction everywhere we turn, stem from a deeply rooted emotional battle with the orphan spirit. For our yeas to be yeas and our nays to be nays, we need to uproot this spirit from our lives. We must come to understand we are irrevocably accepted in the Beloved, that Jesus came to reveal to us the heart of His Father, and that God is not mad at us, but instead He is madly in love with us.

As we break free from the bondage of the orphan spirit, God's love for us can be our driving force, our new and central motivation. It will lead us to no longer being reluctant or hesitant to obey God and answer His call. Beloved, we are in a "for such a time as this" season. We cannot afford to get tripped up by beliefs and mindsets that rise up against the knowledge of God's unshakable love for us. You are indeed accepted by God, and there is no mistake He made in that decision.

In the story of Esther, I believe Esther's greatest obstacle was self-preservation rooted in the orphan spirit and that Mordecai used his words of authority to break through that spirit in Esther's life.

CHARACTERISTICS AND SIGNS OF THE ORPHAN SPIRIT

- The orphan spirit entered the planet at the fall of Adam and Eve. God was the center of man's world, and He provided for man and protected everything that He created. The major result of the fall is that man became the center of his own world. He orphaned himself and became alienated from God. When man becomes the center of his own universe, he becomes his own resource and becomes afraid of God.

- Spiritual orphans lack emotional identity and attempt to earn a sense of identity through their efforts. Spiritual orphans are those who feel alone, who feel they do not have a safe and secure place in the Father's heart where He can affirm, protect, provide, and express His love to them. They feel as if they do not belong. They are full of fear, anxiety, and insecurity. Spiritual orphans have an independent spirit that often causes them to hide or deny pain.

- The orphan spirit is always concerned with provision and protection. This worry causes them to operate in their own abilities, apart from God. The orphan spirit moves out of self-sufficiency, creating fig leaves to protect itself against the Creator and hide.

- A person who operates out of an orphan spirit constantly harbors feelings of abandonment, loneliness, alienation, and isolation. Esther was isolated and alienated from her family and forced to live in a pagan world. Her peace and security were taken, and she was forced to comply to survive. Those who operate out of an orphan heart never want to rebel against those in authority, for this may jeopardize security.

- The orphan spirit operates out of insecurity and fear. When Esther was not summoned for thirty days, she did not know if the king had found someone more pleasing or if she was merely losing her influence. Even though Scripture states that the king loved Esther more than all the women in the kingdom, she was not secure in his love. Many times orphans have an inability to receive love.

- The orphan spirit causes you to be performance oriented. Esther won favor with the king. "When the turn came for Esther (the young woman Mordecai had adopted, the daughter of his uncle Abihail) to go to the king, she asked for nothing other than what Hegai, the king's eunuch who was in charge of the harem, suggested. And Esther won the favor of everyone who saw her" (Est. 2:15, NIV). When we take a look at this scripture in the NIV translation, it says Esther "won the favor," indicating that favor wasn't just given or bestowed upon her; favor came because of something she was doing. I believe Esther was gracious and well-mannered, but her heart was one that believed, "I have to perform or give it everything I have to become number one."

- The orphan spirit causes you to always be in an inner competition with others. This spirit dictates that you must stand out at all costs.

The orphan spirit gains its identity from being better than everyone else.

- The orphan spirit lacks self-esteem and identity.

- The orphan spirit is self-reliant. When family life is dramatically disrupted, orphans will depend only on what they can control.

- The orphan spirit is self-protecting. Orphans feel unsure about their position. They feel uncovered and unprotected; therefore the instinct is to protect themselves.

- The orphan spirit is deeply rooted in self-preservation. Self-preservation is an obsession with protecting the things you are afraid of losing. Mordecai challenges Esther's fear of losing everything she had worked so hard to gain. Ironically when we become obsessed with protecting the very things we are afraid of losing, we tend to lose them more quickly. Mark 8:34–35 says, "Then he called the crowd to him along with his disciples and said: 'Whoever wants to be my disciple must deny themselves and take up their cross and follow me. For whoever wants to save their life will lose it, but whoever loses their life for me and for the gospel will save it'" (NIV).

DELIVERANCE FROM THE ORPHAN SPIRIT

Only after fasting and praying did Esther become confident and take on a leadership role in the story. After fasting, prayer, and deliverance from an orphan spirit, Esther, "initially a beautiful young woman with a weak character...becomes transformed into a person with heroic moral stature and political skill."[1]

I believe that in the time of fasting and prayer the Lord delivered her from the bondage of an orphan spirit. This is how we can explain Esther's abrupt change in behavior from deep despair to determined action and from passiveness to leadership. She found confidence in the presence of the Lord. During her fast "Esther connected with her inner self and understood why she had been made queen. She understood why she had to suffer through her relationship with this irritable king. She understood that she had a mission and that she could shape reality rather than passively suffer through it. Esther had been made queen to save her people; her mission and her faith shaped her character and inspired her to act and succeed."[2]

Throughout our lives we all face crises from time to time. Sometimes the crises are severe, threatening our stability and security. In this time our true identities are tested and perfected. We must embrace the Father's love and acceptance. We are a peculiar people, a chosen generation. We are children of the King and heirs to all the promises of God. He has already declared the end from the beginning; His plans for us are good and not evil. We must be healed from "Father rejection." We are not orphans. We have received the spirit of adoption, and we can cry out to Him,

"Abba, Father." God the Father's love protects and sustains us on our chosen paths and for such a time as this.

PRAYER THAT BREAKS THE ORPHAN SPIRIT

Lord, I thank You that You love me. I receive Your love. Let the power of Your blood cleanse me from an orphan heart. Baptize my heart with the fire of Your love. Let the fire of Your love burn away the rejection and fear. Let the fire of Your love purge away the dross of the orphan spirit. Your love is like vehement flames, and many waters cannot quench Your love for me. The flames of Your love for me are eternal, and many floods will never be able to drown it out. Your Word says that You will not leave us as orphans, but You will come to us.

Holy Spirit, come and pour the love of God in my heart. Holy Spirit, teach me how to receive the love of the Father. Come empower me with the truth of Your love. I loose myself from the survivalist mentality. I don't want to just survive; I want to enjoy the abundant life You have for me. I am tired of making fig leaves for myself. I am tired of living in fear and shame. I will no longer hide from Your presence.

I humble myself, Lord. I choose to die to self. Your Word says unless a kernel of wheat falls to the ground and dies, it will not bear fruit. I will not only be concerned with my best interests, but I use my authority to benefit the well-being of others. I shake myself free from passivity and indifference.

I am a child of the King. I am not an orphan. I don't have to perform to receive Your love. I received the spirit of adoption, and I cry, "Abba, Father." I loose myself from all insecurity and fear. I loose myself from self-preservation.

Forgive me for being obsessed with trying to keep things I've obtained through striving and competing. No longer will I compete to survive. I have favor with You. I trust Your love to protect me. I find my security in You. You are my heavenly Father; You provide for me. I choose to obey Your Word. I will no longer try to save my life but lose it in the arms of Your love. Amen.

GET THE RIGHT MENTORS

Sometimes your life has gotten off track because you have not had the proper mentors. You've served kingdoms, systems, and people who have not poured into your life properly, but I'm decreeing that God will put the right people in your life who will pour into you. Do you know you can get one revelation from someone that can catapult you to the next place?

I have visited fifty-three countries. I have visited all types of churches and seen all types of things. Why? Because Apostle John Eckhardt saw a grace on my life. He pulled me up and poured into me. He laid his hands on me and said, "You will travel to nations, and not only will you travel to nations; you will stand and preach." Then he extended his platform to me and let me preach. He trained me as my mentor.

Some of you need someone to speak to your womanhood or your manhood. You need someone to give to you and pour into you, sharing his or her platform and correcting and helping you perfect your calling. There are things I didn't have to walk through because someone poured into me.

The kingdom of God is about discipleship. The kingdom of God is about reproduction.

Some of us listen to the same voices all the time. We may say, "I'm a Word of Faith person. I'm going to stay with the Word of Faith," or "I'm apostolic, so I'm going to stay with the apostolic." But we need to be open to new voices, seasoned men and women of God who have tapped into the new things, the now things God is doing.

I think about how Esther had Mordecai. Mordecai challenged Esther because he knew she had an orphan spirit, a survivalist mentality. He challenged this spirit within her when he said, "Listen, don't you think you will survive. Not only will you perish, but you *and* your people will perish. But deliverance and expansion will come if you step up and use the position God has put you in."

Esther had a drawback spirit, but as your mentor from a distance I want to challenge you not to draw back but to pursue the destiny and purpose God has for you, to overtake the enemy, and to recover all that has been lost.

We need someone to challenge us, and I believe you will meet the right people who will take you to a new level of glory and grace. I pray right now that you will learn to stand up in your anointing, that God will put people near you who will catapult you. I pray that negative people will be removed from your life. Let this be a day that God will begin to align you for your assignment. May you be bold in your self-evaluation and unafraid to ask the hard questions: "How am I aligned? What am I doing with my time?" You get aligned by your decisions, and time is so important. It is the measurement of life. So I pray that God will continue to teach you to number your days so that you may gain a heart of wisdom so that each day is maximized and set up for victory. May you always be one step ahead and your enemies far behind, in Jesus' name.

Chapter 7

THE CHOSEN ARE FILLED
WITH THE KNOWLEDGE
OF GOD'S WILL

[We] do not cease to pray for you, and to ask that you
may be filled with the knowledge of His will in all wisdom
and spiritual understanding; that you may walk worthy
of the Lord, fully pleasing Him, being fruitful in every
good work and increasing in the knowledge of God;
strengthened with all might, according to His glorious
power, for all patience and longsuffering with joy.
—COLOSSIANS 1:9–11

OST BELIEVERS UNDERSTAND that they are called, but what most may not understand is that the calling is just an invitation. The next level is to become chosen, which is predicated upon how you respond to the invitation. God has already chosen you, but your choice to follow Him completely is yours alone. This is the beauty of free will and the power of choice. God created you to know Him and to have an intimate relationship with Him. How do you respond to the calling of God as He calls you to something bigger than yourself? What *you* decide indicates whether you are just one of those who received the invitation or if you are one who received the invitation and accepted it.

We must remember that God doesn't sift through humanity and choose one person over the other. God is not a respecter of persons. He doesn't gather us all together like a sea of humanity and say, "I choose this one. I choose that one." No. Being chosen depends on what we do. The decisions we make. The sacrifices we make. How we move toward God. How we partner with heaven. How do we connect with heaven to do what heaven has designed us to do?

In reality many of us don't do what's necessary to walk in the fullness of our calling. But the chosen life is made up of choices that shape a chosen destiny, that release the blessing and favor of God in our lives, and that call us to a special place in God where He can trust us with the riches and glory of heaven. God has an expected end for our lives. He has an expectation for how our lives will lead to that expected end. If we want to stay on the chosen path, we cannot live our lives any way we want to.

The chosen love the presence of God for this reason: He gives direction and revelation on how to live a chosen life to those who commit to inquire at His throne. We have to get back to inquiring of God what His will is for our lives. We need revelation. We need understanding. God wants to enlighten the eyes of your understanding. He wants our hearts to be flooded with light. He said, "Call to Me, and

I will answer you, and show you great and mighty things, which you do not know" (Jer. 33:3).

NINE CHARACTERISTICS OF GLORY CARRIERS

We need to know the will of God for our lives in order to walk circumspectly on the path He has ordained. In Colossians 1:9–14 the apostle Paul prayed this prayer for the believers in the first century:

> For this reason we also, since the day we heard it, do not cease to pray for you, and to ask that you may be filled with the knowledge of His will in all wisdom and spiritual understanding; that you may walk worthy of the Lord, fully pleasing Him, being fruitful in every good work and increasing in the knowledge of God; strengthened with all might, according to His glorious power, for all patience and longsuffering with joy; giving thanks to the Father who has qualified us to be partakers of the inheritance of the saints in the light. He has delivered us from the power of darkness and conveyed us into the kingdom of the Son of His love, in whom we have redemption through His blood, the forgiveness of sins.

This passage reveals nine characteristics of what God wants for all those who will carry His glory even until the present day and into the future. They are all connected with how His will is to be the overarching driver for the chosen life.

1. Filled with the knowledge of His will

When we don't understand God's will for our lives, we can't submit to it. We may pray, "Not my will but Yours be done," and not have a clue as to what God's will is. It's common for us to talk about humbly submitting ourselves to God, but how can we do that without being filled with the knowledge of His will? The word *knowledge* is not just about an intellectual knowing. It is about being intimately acquainted. God wants you to have an intimate knowledge of His will for your life, your church, your family, and for every region on the earth He has set for you to occupy.

Once you know the will of God—once God reveals it to you through a dream, vision, or prophetic word—you have the responsibility to submit your entire life to it. Once the will of God has been made known to you, then it becomes the vision for your life. Many of us are perishing for a lack of knowledge of the will of God for our lives. We are perishing because we don't have vision. The Bible says that where there is no vision, people cast off restraint (Prov. 29:18). A clear vision for what God has planned for us is what restrains us from living any kind of way and being easy prey to the enemy. It causes every other will to submit to the will of God. This is why the apostle Paul could say, "It is no longer I who lives, but Christ lives in me" (Gal. 2:20). He said, "For I determined to know nothing among you except Jesus Christ, and Him crucified" (1 Cor. 2:2, NASB).

God is saying that if we're going to live as chosen ones, we must be men and women of God who submit to the will of God. We must determine to know nothing but Jesus Christ and Him crucified. We can begin to cry out even now, "God, fill me with the knowledge of Your will. May every other will submit to the will of God. Everything that I want to do I submit to You. God, give me Your will for my life."

These are the days when we cannot just be in the acceptable or permissive will. We must want the perfect will of God and progress with it as it progresses. We should not get stuck in the past or with yesterday's word. God is always doing something new. The Word of the Lord is living and active (Heb. 4:12). Some of us are stuck because we heard God speak at one season in our lives, but we've not sought Him out for what He is doing in the next season. He says, "Behold, I will do a new thing, now it shall spring forth; shall you not know it?" (Isa. 43:19).

As chosen ones we must continually keep a seeking heart. We must always seek after the Lord to hear from Him what His will is in this season. The Bible tells us, "Blessed are those who hunger and thirst for righteousness, for they shall be filled" (Matt. 5:6). We are supposed to seek first the kingdom and all His righteousness, and everything else will be added to us (Matt. 6:33). We must put the will of God back in first place.

The Bible tells us that we should love the Lord God with all our hearts, souls, minds, and strength (Mark 12:30). Our souls are made up of our minds, wills, and emotions. This verse is telling us that everything that makes up who we are we must submit to the will of God. The chosen are men and women of God who walk according to the perfect will of God—and then we are to be filled with it. To be full means to be "complete especially in detail, number, or duration"; "having all distinguishing characteristics: enjoying all authorized rights and privileges"; "not lacking in any essential: perfect"; or "being at the highest or greatest degree: maximum."[1] When we are filled with the knowledge of God's will, there is no room for anything else. We are not lacking, needing, or left wanting anything else. We are complete, perfect, maxed out.

2. In all wisdom

We need the wisdom of God, not wisdom that is earthly, sensual, and devilish, but wisdom that is pure—wisdom that comes from the presence of God. Wisdom allows us to know how to execute the will of God and to discern the right next thing to do. Wisdom is the ability to apply good sense and sound judgment when it comes to making decisions that will keep us in line with our purpose and destiny. Solomon prayed that God would give him wisdom and teach him how to govern the kingdom. God was so pleased with his cry that not only did He give him wisdom and understanding, but He also gave him so much money until he was the richest man on earth.

God is resourcing His chosen ones with great wealth, great strategy, and great wisdom. Wealth and strategy mean nothing in the hands of fools. They will be squandered and wasted. God is making a great transfer of wealth—from the wicked to the righteous. The righteous are the chosen ones, the ones who have accepted the call to walk unwaveringly according to the Spirit of God. In their hands the wealth that has been stored up for them will be used to build the kingdom. Wisdom is the necessary piece for carrying out God's will with prudence once we know what it is.

I decree that God will release supernatural wisdom, spiritual wisdom. Solomon had the wisdom of God and prospered. Daniel had the wisdom of God and prospered, even in a heathen nation. May God fill us with the knowledge of His will in all wisdom. We want eternal wisdom. We want wisdom that comes from the glory realm. We want wisdom that comes from the mouth and heart of God. Not earthly wisdom, not sensual and devilish wisdom—we want the wisdom of God.

3. Spiritual understanding

One of the greatest deficits on the earth is the spirit of understanding. Many people don't understand the movings and the dealings of the Spirit. With spiritual understanding, not only are we carnal Christians, but we live in the Spirit, understanding how He moves and works and what our role is in relation to fulfilling His efforts.

Spiritual understanding unlocks the glory realm, and you begin to understand the realm of angels and how they help you accomplish your chosen mandate. You begin to understand the realm of miracles and the gifts of the Spirit and how they testify to God's glory in your life. You begin to understand the demonic realm and your authority to defend the things under your measure of rule. You will understand the prophetic realm, the realm of deliverance and of worship, and the kingdom realm—all parts of the whole when it comes to living according to the perfect will of God.

Spiritual understanding comes with a renewed mind. You are one who is spiritually minded—one who understands that you dwell in the coexisting realm. You understand that heaven's resources are yours now and you don't have to wait until you get to heaven to take advantage of them. With a spirit of understanding, you are no longer carnal. You have the mind of Christ.

If the devil can keep you carnal minded, you will be of no good. You will have enmity with God, and as a chosen one you cannot afford to live outside the presence of God. Spiritual-minded people then have a spiritual calling.

Paul said concerning the Spirit and His gifts, "I will not have you to be ignorant" (1 Cor. 12:1, author's paraphrase). Spiritual ignorance is one of the major hindrances of forward advancement in the kingdom, but I am decreeing that the spirit of deception is broken. I decree that we will be men and women of wisdom who operate with spiritual understanding. We will learn how to move and live and have our beings in the spirit realm, in the name of Jesus.

4. A walk worthy of the Lord

What type of life do you live behind closed doors? See, we may think the secret place is just the place of worship, but the secret place is also the place where you do the things you think nobody will see. Having a walk worthy of the Lord is about integrity. Integrity, as defined by C. S. Lewis, is about "doing the right thing, even when no one is watching."[2]

We want to walk worthy of the Lord and of the cross of Christ and His shed blood. We want to be men and women of integrity who walk worthy of the kingdom and its righteousness. In Ephesians 4:1 Paul said, "I, therefore, the prisoner of the Lord, beseech you to walk worthy of the calling with which you were called." The word *calling* here also refers to our vocation. In the Greek it refers to "the divine invitation to embrace salvation in the kingdom of God."[3]

As the theme of this book confirms, many are called, or invited, but few are chosen, or among those who accept the invitation. We have to walk worthy of who we are as chosen ones. We must take up the charge to be imitators of God, walking in "love, as Christ also has loved us and given Himself for us, an offering and a sacrifice to God for a sweet-smelling aroma" (Eph. 5:2).

Walking worthy of the Lord requires a radical commitment of our will to please God.

5. Fully pleasing Him

Fully pleasing God calls for rebalancing our allegiances. Some of us have allegiance to seemingly good systems, but good and God are not the same thing. Some of us have allegiance to demonic systems. Wherever our loyalties lie, we must ultimately and firstly pledge our allegiance to the Lamb of God. We cannot fear God and man. We cannot love God and money. We cannot serve two masters. We cannot waver between two opinions, between life and death, blessing and cursing. God challenges us, "Choose you this day whom you will serve."

Because we are aiming to be fully pleasing to Him, we must be fully convinced that neither life nor death—that nothing—shall separate us from the love of Christ—not a principality, not a power, not things that are or things to come.

For many believers and unbelievers alike, a big hindrance to pleasing God is people pleasing. Sometimes we live to please others. We want others to pat us on the back and tell us we're doing well. Sometimes we do things just to be seen, to be known, recognized, accepted, and valued by others. But the chosen know that they are accepted in the beloved, that God knows their name and sees them. They find pleasure and satisfaction in living before an audience of One. They have a revelation of the love of the Father, and pleasing Him is their one desire.

The chosen are not puppets and are not moved by traditions of men. We have a commitment to the cross. Jesus Christ is worthy of our commitment and love. We are Jesus lovers. We want to live a life that prophesies to the heavens, and anyplace in our lives that is not pleasing to God we are willing to cut loose.

Just like Daniel, Shadrach, Meshach, and Abednego, we will not bow to the systems and traditions of men. We stand for Christ. He is on the throne of our hearts, and we are sold out to Him. We love what He loves and hate what He hates.

We are those who love God first, and everything we do flows out of our love for God. We prophesy because we love God. We bind the devil because we love God. We are for His plans and purposes, and we want to administrate His kingdom agenda on the earth. So we are not coming against the devil just because the devil is evil. No. We're coming against the devil because God hates him, and that's what the true spirit of the fear of the Lord is—to love what God loves and to hate what He hates. God said that He would rather we be hot or cold (Rev. 3:15–16). The chosen are red hot for the things of God. We are people after His heart.

6. Fruitful in every good work

Many of us may not be fruitful because we are tied to too many systems of men, but when you come to a place and say, "I am going to walk worthy of the Lord, fully pleasing Him," that is when you become fruitful in every good work. This is when the glory comes upon your life and you move into a time of multiplication because you have sold out to God. I am telling you, the days of puppet Christians are over. God is coming to measure and see which branches are producing fruit. Jesus said:

> Abide in Me, and I in you. As the branch cannot bear fruit of itself, unless it abides in the vine, neither can you, unless you abide in Me.
>
> I am the vine, you are the branches. He who abides in Me, and I in him, bears much fruit; for without Me you can do nothing. If anyone does not abide in Me, he is cast out as a branch and is withered; and they gather them and throw them into the fire, and they are burned.
>
> —JOHN 15:4–6

The chosen abide in Christ. We walk worthy and according to the Spirit of God. When we don't abide in Christ—seeking after Him, worshipping Him, studying His Word, and learning His character and attributes to reflect them on the earth—we cease to be fruitful and multiply.

These are days when those who have a heart for God and are really running for Him will be catapulted from their ordinary into His extraordinary. He's getting ready to release His power over your life so that you will be fruitful in every good work.

Perhaps you've spent years serving in the background, but because you have been abiding in the vine, God is moving you to the forefront. God is increasing you in every good work. You will be fruitful. Maybe you have been sowing and sowing, and you're not seeing the fullness of what God is getting ready to do. God is breaking the law of diminished returns, and where you sow a lot and only get a few returns, you will begin to see an increase in your harvest. Let this be a season of great fruitfulness.

I declare also that as you seek after fruitfulness, in the light of God's glory, you will get clarity to know the will of God for your life. If you are doing a work, and it is not fruitful, maybe it is not what God has designed you to do. Therefore, I decree that this be a time for self-examination—a time when God will cause you to examine your motives and the things He has designed you to do. Get ready to ask yourself, "Why am I doing what I'm doing? Is it a plan from man, or is it because I'm just a great administrator?" Get your journal out, open up the Word of God, open up the portals of heaven through prayer, and seek God for a revelation on what you have been called to do. God takes great pleasure in the prosperity of His chosen. Your fruitfulness pleases Him.

I decree that your work will be tried in the fire and only pure gold will come forth so that you can move forward and advance the kingdom.

7. Increasing in the knowledge of God

Not only are we going to be fully pleasing to Him, fruitful in every good work, but we are also going to increase in the knowledge of God. This is the hour, beloved, that we must know God. For the Lord says, "The people who know their God shall be strong, and carry out great exploits" (Dan. 11:32).

The glory realm shows us the picture of who God is. You may have a measure of the knowledge of God, but God is full of wisdom. He is so great that His greatness is unsearchable. We can never exhaust what we know about God. We can always increase in our knowledge of the heart and ways of God. We can always get to know Him more intimately so that even when you worship or sit down to study, a canopy of glory will drop down on you, illuminating the character of God. The more we know God, the more we will love Him. The more we love Him, the more we will obey Him. The more we obey Him, the more we are exposed to His glory, the more we will see miracles. The more miracles that we see, the more we will see the kingdom expand and lives and communities transformed. The miracle realm testifies to God's glory and saving power.

We are going to be a generation that will not get enough of the knowledge and presence of God. It is an atrocity that, even among believers, some know about God but don't know Him for themselves.

When was the last time you heard a message preached about Jesus Christ? When was the last time you preached a message on the knowledge of God or the ways of God or the movings of God? When was the last time you studied the attributes of God? These are the days when we must press in to know God, to know Him for ourselves. We will become unstoppable when we are in the center of His will, when we have increased in His knowledge, and when we understand His ways.

8. Strengthened with all might

As you get to know God, you will be strengthened with all might according to His glorious power. Strength comes from knowing God. You become strengthened in the power of His might.

The spirit of might is a force. When this force comes upon you, a new level of confidence and authority comes because you have gone through the process of coming into the knowledge of God's will. You've let God remove all your false allegiances. You've made some determinations in your heart about which path you will follow. Now you need strength to live it out.

Matthew 25 talks about the parables of the wise and foolish virgins. The foolish virgins had no oil in their lamps, but the wise virgins did. The bridegroom was late, and they didn't know when he would come, so they all went to sleep. When the bridegroom came, the wise virgins were ready. If you put it in a spiritual context, they were ready to move with God.

I am telling you, chosen one, we are going to be oily in the spirit. We are going to have the oil of the Spirit. We are going to move to a place where we are strengthened with all might. The power of God rests upon us. We are going to be like wise virgins with our oil held even in reserve. We are going to keep our lamps trimmed and burning. We are on fire for God, and our zeal will not burn out.

9. Patient endurance

Because American culture is an *instant* society, too many Christians have come to expect a microwave-like experience with God, but certain things are going to take time. I don't care how much activation and revelation you get— some things will just have to come as you mature in the things of God. We can pray for the patience and endurance to wait on God, and we can look forward to the joy that is set before us. When we wait on God, He pours a measure of strength into our hearts. The psalmist said, "Wait on the LORD; be of good courage, and He shall strengthen your heart; wait, I say, on the LORD!" (Ps. 27:14). We also know that the joy of the Lord released to us is our strength.

I pray that you will be strengthened with all might, that even as you wait for certain things to manifest in your life, you will be overwhelmed with joy and gratitude and will begin to take your focus off of yourself and start pressing in to God. Beloved, an entire glory realm is being opened to you. What a privilege you carry that you would be qualified to be a partaker of the inheritance of the saints and the light, being delivered from all darkness because Christ has delivered us from the kingdom of darkness and put us in the kingdom of light.

These are our chosen mandates concerning the will of God for us. I challenge you to take this passage of Scripture, Colossians 1:9–14, and pray it, meditate over it, and decree it over your life. I challenge you to press in to God to know His will. You have an open invitation into the throne of God.

INQUIRING OF THE LORD

Before we leave this chapter, I want to share with you something the Lord has been talking to me about concerning the open heaven and mantles of wisdom and revelation. There is such a divine interaction between heaven and earth happening in this season. God's people are seeking Him, and He is answering. In 1 Samuel 30:8 David begins to inquire of the Lord, and I believe this is such a season where we really have to restore the art of inquiring of the Lord. We need to restore the practice of stopping our lives, being still, and asking God for wisdom and revelation—fresh wisdom and strategies.

The Lord is shifting us into our primary assignment. He is giving revelation that will change our situations, if only we will humble ourselves. We must do this before the Lord so we can hear. God really wants us to pursue Him, but knowing how to carry out what He reveals will take divine strategy. It will take our coming together under an open heaven, which we create through prayer, humility, and worship.

We really need to inquire of the Lord to get knowledge and revelation of His will so we won't fight with the wrong enemy, waste resources, and wind up in the wrong place at the wrong time. We need to inquire of the Lord about our relationships and where we should be and what we should be doing while we are there.

God is stirring up and breaking up certain things and certain relationships that cannot go where we are going. It's not that they are bad people; it's not that they are not saved people, but certain people will be in your life as Lot was to Abraham. Certain people and certain relationships must end because they will hinder you and stifle your growth. But God will connect us with new people—people we never thought we would be in covenant with—and they will bless us and be like iron against our iron, sharpening us for strategic purposes.

Lifelong covenant relationships are being released in this hour, but we must begin to inquire of the Lord. We cannot let the enemy get us over into presumption, where we imitate the faith actions of others without having the word given to us and God quickening the word of life inside of us.

If you are going to fulfill your destiny and walk in the full knowledge of God's will, you must obey God. We must do everything He tells us to do, the way He tells us to do it, and with the people He tells us to do it with. That's why the season is here that God is purifying our hearts. We hear God through our hearts. This is why He says, "I take out the stony heart and put in a heart of flesh." He is taking out all unrighteousness and impure thoughts and motives. In turn He is causing the spirit of revelation to rest upon us.

He's revealing Himself to us—His patterns and strategies. Sometimes we get caught up in the details of what God has asked us to do. Listen, I may not know the name, but I know what it looks like when I see it. That's where God wants to take us. Sometimes we want the exact name of the thing, but what God wants is faith. Where you say, "Lord, I don't know the name of it, but I know the way. I know which way to go because You're the way, the truth, and the life. When I get there, I'm going to see it," that's the kind of faith God needs us to have because if we know God, we can trust Him without knowing every detail as if we have some measure of control beyond His. We do not. Our lives are His, and He is in control.

When we begin to do things in the flesh, start fighting our own wars and building our own empires, we miss out on the true focus God has in mind for our gifts. What about the people in your sphere of influence who are attached to your anointing? It is such a season for us to pursue righteousness and be righteous with God's people—the ones we have been assigned to. Like Solomon, we need to ask God for strategies: "God, how do I lead Your people? How do I use my gifts to bless those You've put in my life?"

How many times do we make decisions out of our flesh? God had to teach me too. We can say one word the wrong way to people and create a domino effect where we throw their lives out of the trajectory and sequence of God. We must move and live and operate by the Spirit.

As we come to the throne room to inquire of the Lord, we need to remind ourselves of His eternality, omniscience, and power. God knows everything and is omnipresent. He is everywhere at the same time. There has never been a time that God was not. He's already been in your future. He knows everything. When you get reminded of these attributes of God, you gain strength. You build yourself up in your most holy of faith, and then you can hear God.

That's why God says, "Fret not yourself because of evil-doers" (Ps. 37:1, AMPC). If you're fretting, you can't hear.

Then, as you hear God say, "Here is the way; walk in it," posture yourself and purpose in your heart to obey Him. I keep repeating this because it is so important. One of the pitfalls of the prophetic is that people don't always lean in to their prophecy and start doing it.

What I used to do sometimes was just kind of wait. I knew what God had said, but I wanted to pray over it and make decrees. I would birth it in the spirit, but then there comes a time when we all have to lean in to our prophecy and do it. Has God told you, "I've called you to write books"? Well, at some point you will have to sit down and start writing books. If God is saying, "I want you to prosper and be in good health," you will need to go to a class and learn how to eat right. You will need to go to the gym. When you get a prophetic word, some-times you have to make what my husband calls a SWOT analysis—you have to look at your strengths, weaknesses, opportunities, and threats. You'll need to assess where you are so you can move forward and begin to make decisions to move forward in your destiny.

God wants to give you revelation of your life and impart to you a spirit of wisdom. He wants to give you the keys that will unlock your destiny and mysteries and truth as you've never known before. Pursue your purpose from a place of inquiry, where you get a real strategy and not an unction or inkling. Inquire of the Lord and get real clarity. Don't you move until you get clarity. This is not the season for missteps.

God is going to give you so much clarity. I decree that there will be no more confusion about who you are, but you will see, you will know, you will consider, and you will understand what the will of the Lord is for your life.

Chapter 8

ANGELS ASSIGNED TO YOUR DESTINY

For He shall give His angels charge over you, to keep you in all your ways.
—PSALM 91:11

THERE IS A new assignment of angels where God is releasing angels all around us—angels that will connect us with our destiny. I call them angels of destiny. They are assigned to the prophetic word over your life, and they help you fulfill it. The Bible calls them "ministering spirits sent forth to minister for those who will inherit salvation" (Heb. 1:14).

Angels have been assigned to all of us to help us get across to our next season in life. Many of God's chosen have been receiving prophecies about promotion, and when there's promotion, there's always an adversary that wants to stop us from going through the door. But God is releasing a new force, a new company of angels that will be governed by the Holy Spirit to break you through. They will war with you, protect you, and bring you to that place of new beginnings.

During my prayer and study time God has continued to put images of angels before my eyes. He keeps challenging me to study them. He's been showing me that He is doing something new with angels on behalf of the chosen. He is reintroducing us to a whole company of supernatural agents on call to do our bidding. To get them to act on our command, we must speak what God is speaking. Our actions and instructions to them must be in line with God's will. Angels are not genies, and they are not subject to flesh. This is why it is so important that we walk according to the Spirit and in the knowledge of God's will for our lives.

As we pursue God and press in to the Spirit, the Lord will begin to give us revelations about the natural army—you and me—and the spiritual army—the angelic host of heaven—moving together. What we see with this collaboration is a picture of the natural and the spiritual converging in the coexisting spirit realm.

In this chapter I want to show you how to stir up the angelic spirits sent to minister to us and the various roles they play in the lives of the chosen.

> The angel of the LORD encamps all around those who fear Him, and delivers them.
>
> —PSALM 34:7

DISPENSING ANGELS THROUGH
PRAISE AND WORSHIP

When I would see angels, the Lord would tell me to lift up my voice in praise and worship. "You are dispensing the angels," He'd say. He was helping me understand that praise and worship are how we release angels to set up ambushes against our enemies. We forget that at times, but when we open up our mouths and praise the Lord, angels start moving on our behalf.

This is exactly what the Lord did in 2 Chronicles 20:21–22 when King Jehoshaphat and the people of Israel were facing a mighty army where their defeat was inevitable in the natural. They sought the Lord about what they should do. Here is the word from the king:

> And when he had consulted with the people, he appointed those who should sing to the LORD, and who should praise the beauty of holiness, as they went out before the army and were saying: "Praise the LORD, for His mercy endures forever."

This was the outcome:

> Now when they began to sing and to praise, the LORD set ambushes against the people of Ammon, Moab, and Mount Seir, who had come against Judah; and they were defeated.

The account says that "the LORD set ambushes." But I believe by the Spirit of God, God dispensed angels to do this work. Their praise moved the hand of God, who then dispatched angels to set ambushes against their enemies.

We see that when they began to praise and magnify the Lord, compassion for their predicament rose up before Him and He was compelled to act.

In another example, two of God's chosen apostles, Paul and Silas, were in prison for preaching the gospel and casting out demons. Late into the night Paul and Silas began to pray and sing hymns to the Lord. "Suddenly there was a great earthquake, so that the foundations of the prison were shaken; and immediately all the doors were opened and everyone's chains were loosed" (Acts 16:26). I believe this to be another angelic intervention, which eventually led to many lives being saved into the kingdom of God.

The Lord has been saying to me, "Tell My people I am releasing a new company of angels, angels of My presence. These are the angels of your destiny." Certain angels will move with you, but others will be assigned to your specific assignment. They are door-opening, chain-breaking, earthshaking, ambush-setting angels who will be released when you open your mouth in prayer, praise, and worship before the Lord and in the face of your enemies.

Do you remember in Acts 12 when Peter was in prison? The church kept a 24/7 prayer vigil going on his behalf. As they prayed, the hinges of the prison doors blew off, and the angel of the Lord came and said, "'Arise quickly!' And his chains fell off his hands. Then the angel said to him, 'Gird yourself and tie on your sandals'; and so he did. And he said to him, 'Put on your garment and follow me'" (Acts 12:7–8). Step by step the angel was with Peter, shielding him from being spotted by the guards, telling him which direction to walk in, and clearing all exits until he was safely out.

God is getting ready to blow some hinges off some doors. When you learn how to praise Him and say, "The Lord is good, and His mercy endures forever," and when you can say, "O God, we bless You," even as the enemy is coming against you like a flood, you will see God release His angels to encamp around you and miraculously deliver you back onto your chosen path.

Let's now get familiar with the company of angels God has made available to us.

THE FUNCTIONS OF THE ANGELIC REALM

Psalm 103:20 tells us that angels hearken to the voice of God's word. Angels excel in strength. Angels are powerful spirits that have been sent to assist us in advancing the kingdom. Though it can be hard to realize, it is important to know that we are not alone. First, God has given us His Spirit to comfort, guide, teach, and empower us for our chosen assignments, but we also have the ministry of angels, which have been sent forth from the throne of God to minster on our behalf. They give us supernatural assistance.

Many who hear the word of the Lord spoken over their lives wonder how His word can manifest in their lives. Have you ever received a prophetic word that seems almost impossible? God has assigned angels to make it so. They help fulfill His divine purposes. When we speak and decree the word of the Lord, angels begin to minister on our behalf.

Angels are at work behind the scenes, influencing cities, nations, governments, and history, and as we've discovered, they are also sent to minister on behalf of individuals.

And yes, angels are involved in helping you fulfill your destiny and purpose.

In Genesis 28:12 Jacob saw a portal through which angels were ascending and descending. This portal is Bethel, the house of God and the gate of heaven. The house of God today is the church. We are now Bethel.

A portal to heaven opens up when we pray, praise, worship, preach, and prophesy. Angels ascend and descend through this portal. They are sent to help and assist us. I will discuss the open heavens in more depth in chapter 9, but I wanted to touch on it here so that you can see them in the context of how angels function.

THE MINISTRIES OF ANGELS

Angels are connected to God's chosen prophets and prophetic people. Jacob encountered a host of angels in Genesis 32:1–2 (KJV):

> And Jacob went on his way, and the angels of God
> met him. And when Jacob saw them, he said, This
> is God's host: and he called the name of that place
> Mahanaim.

Here the angels were assigned to bring Jacob to his designated place. In other words, angels were a part of him fulfilling his destiny. Mahanaim in that verse means "two camps."[1] This was an angelic army sent to assist Jacob.

The prophetic word reveals and releases destiny. God has a destiny for each person, and we are responsible to discover it, pursue it, and walk in it. Angelic assistance includes angels that go before us and angels that protect us. They assist us against human and demonic opposition.

They assist us in overcoming resistance to the fulfillment of His word.

> The chariots of God are twenty thousand, even thousands of angels: the Lord is among them, as in Sinai, in the holy place.
>
> —Psalm 68:17, kjv

Angels were instrumental in the giving of the Law. They were involved in the establishment of the covenant between God and His people. Angels are always involved with God's covenant people. Those in covenant with God are not alone. We are not left to our own strength in fulfilling the word of the Lord.

> ...who maketh his angels spirits; his ministers a flaming fire.
>
> —Psalm 104:4, kjv

Angels are spirits. They operate in the invisible realm. They are spiritual beings that respond to the word of the Lord. They respond to prayer, praise, worship, fasting, preaching, and prophecy. Spirits respond to spiritual activities.

> And I will send an angel before thee; and I will drive out the Canaanite, the Amorite, and the Hittite, and the Perizzite, the Hivite, and the Jebusite.
>
> —Exodus 33:2, kjv

Angels go before us to drive out the enemy. They go before us to make way for us to possess our possessions.

The word of the Lord is often a declaration of what belongs to us. We are not alone in trying to possess it.

Angels help provide significant breakthroughs. Angels help us overcome impossible odds. Angels help us overcome giants and strong enemies.

ANGELS ARE ACTIVATED BY THE WORD OF THE LORD

As I said near the beginning of this chapter, once the word of destiny or prophecy is spoken, angels are released to help fulfill it. The word of the Lord initiates the activity of angels in our lives. I also believe that different angels can be assigned from heaven to us at different times.

> So shall my word be that goeth forth out of my mouth: it shall not return unto me void, but it shall accomplish that which I please, and it shall prosper in the thing whereto I sent it.
> —ISAIAH 55:11, KJV

> And he said unto me, The LORD, before whom I walk, will send his angel with thee, and prosper thy way; and thou shalt take a wife for my son of my kindred, and of my father's house.
> —GENESIS 24:40, KJV

Prosper means to succeed or flourish. God's word will prosper or succeed where it is sent. Angels can be sent before us to prosper our way. We can also prosper through prophesying (Ezra 6:14).

Prophetic intercession and prophetic utterances are instrumental in releasing the ministry of angels. God is committed to performing His word on behalf of His chosen ones, and He sends His angels to assist in its performance.

> That confirmeth the word of his servant, and performeth the counsel of his messengers; that saith to Jerusalem, Thou shalt be inhabited; and to the cities of Judah, Ye shall be built, and I will raise up the decayed places thereof.
> —ISAIAH 44:26, KJV

God performs the counsel of His messengers. His messengers were the prophets. God is committed to His word, and He sends angels to cause it to come to pass.

> Then said the LORD unto me, Thou hast well seen: for I will hasten my word to perform it.
> —JEREMIAH 1:12, KJV

I love this verse of Scripture. God watches over His word to perform it. Angels excel in strength to do the will of God. God has made them strong for this purpose. Angels are involved in what God's messengers speak. We do not have the strength or wisdom to do the great things of which God speaks. Man is limited in his power and ability to perform the counsel of God. We are dependent upon heaven and its resources.

We can trust God to release His angels on our behalf when we speak and walk in His counsel. Angels are given charge over us. In other words, they are appointed over us. They assist us and protect us as we walk in God's purpose for our lives.

> For he shall give his angels charge over thee, to keep
> thee in all thy ways.
>
> —PSALM 91:11, KJV

Angels delight in hearing and fulfilling God's prophetic word. Angels take pleasure in assisting us in fulfilling God's plans. They continually wait on God and His
people. Angels love God's word, and they love performing
it. Angels love God's presence, and they love to praise and
worship Him.

> Be not forgetful to entertain strangers: for thereby
> some have entertained angels unawares.
>
> —HEBREWS 13:2, KJV

Angels visit our services, and it is possible that they
have been there in the form of humans without our being
aware.

Strong worship is an atmosphere for angels and the
chosen. Heaven drops (Hebrew word *nataph* meaning "to
prophesy"[2]) at the presence of God (Ps. 68:8). As we know,
the chosen also love God's presence and His word. Angels
join us in our worship. They also listen to the word of the
Lord.

> Unto whom it was revealed, that not unto them-
> selves, but unto us they did minister the things,
> which are now reported unto you by them that have
> preached the gospel unto you with the Holy Ghost
> sent down from heaven; which things the angels
> desire to look into.
>
> —1 PETER 1:12, KJV

Angels have a great desire to look into the things of which God speaks. They are interested in His prophetic plans and seeing them come to pass. I believe they rejoice at the fulfillment of His word.

Angels often stand behind prophets and ministry gifts when they are preaching. We have seen this many times in our services. Angels often stand on the platform. They are involved in what we are preaching and declaring.

> Behold, I send an Angel before thee, to keep thee
> in the way, and to bring thee into the place which
> I have prepared. Beware of him, and obey his voice,
> provoke him not; for he will not pardon your trans-
> gressions: for my name is in him. But if thou shalt
> indeed obey his voice, and do all that I speak; then I
> will be an enemy unto thine enemies, and an adver-
> sary unto thine adversaries.
> —Exodus 23:20–22, KJV

DISOBEDIENCE CAN PROVOKE ANGELS

Angels can even be provoked. God warned Israel not to provoke the angel sent before it. Disobedience to the word and voice of the Lord can provoke angels. "Provoke" is the Hebrew word *marar*, meaning "to make bitter" or "to be enraged."[3] This is a sobering thought. Angels don't like it when God's word is disobeyed. Angels place high honor on the word of the Lord. They are committed to God and His Word.

> And Elisha prayed, and said, LORD, I pray thee, open
> his eyes, that he may see. And the LORD opened the
> eyes of the young man; and he saw: and, behold,

the mountain was full of horses and chariots of fire
round about Elisha.

—2 KINGS 6:17, KJV

Angels are therefore absolutely committed to God's
word and seeing it come to pass. They are faithful servants of God and faithful to us as well when we walk in
and obey God's word. The prophet Elisha was aware of the
heavenly host and prayed for God to open the eyes of his
servant.

The Lord also opened the eyes of Balaam to see an angel
in the way (Num. 22:31). This angel was sent to withstand
Balaam, who was called by Balak to curse Israel. Balaam
was spared and prophesied blessing over Israel, which
enraged Balak.

We don't want to provoke angels. We want them on our
side, assisting us. They make great helpers but are formi-
dable enemies. When we submit to God's prophetic purposes, they will be our friends and not our enemies. They
will help us succeed and fulfill God's prophetic word and
plan for our lives.

ANGELS ASSIST IN CARRYING OUT GOD'S JUDGMENTS

And immediately the angel of the Lord smote him,
because he gave not God the glory: and he was eaten
of worms, and gave up the ghost.

—ACTS 12:23, KJV

When prophets prophesy judgment, then angels can be
released to fulfill them. Angels assist in carrying out
God's judgments. Individuals and nations can come under

judgments executed by angels. God watches over His word to perform it. God can use human armies and angelic armies to release judgments. Angels are involved in the judgments released in the Book of Revelation.

> For I will defend this city, to save it, for mine own sake, and for my servant David's sake. And it came to pass that night, that the angel of the LORD went out, and smote in the camp of the Assyrians an hundred fourscore and five thousand: and when they arose early in the morning, behold, they were all dead corpses. So Sennacherib king of Assyria departed, and went and returned, and dwelt at Nineveh.
>
> —2 KINGS 19:34–36, KJV

An angel destroyed the camp of the Assyrians after Isaiah released the word of the Lord to Hezekiah. This was an immediate fulfillment. This again shows the power of angels and their obedience to the word of the Lord.

The chosen are connected to the angelic realm. The invisible realm responds to our commands as we align with the will of God. Our words are spirit and life and the spiritual containers of the will and purposes of God. It is important that we grow in our understanding of how the angelic realm serves us.

I decree now that the heavens be opened and angels be released as God has commanded. I loose angels to ascend and descend the ladder to the gates of heaven on our behalf. I loose angelic protection over the lives and assignments of God's chosen. I decree that we will hear the voice of destiny pulling us forward and that destiny angels will be with us. I decree that angels will connect us to our destiny and people who will help us along the way. I loose angels of prosperity and promotion, destiny and purpose to minister to us in this season.

Chapter 9

THE HEART OF THE CHOSEN

*The LORD has sought out a man after his
own heart. The LORD has already appointed
him to be the leader of his people.*
—1 SAMUEL 13:14, NLT

THE CHOSEN ARE people after God's own heart. They mirror His heart of righteousness. The chosen live from the integrity of their hearts. They rely on God to take out their hearts of stone and replace them with hearts of flesh. They long to be transformed from glory to glory. They welcome the purification process. The chosen are not interested in just being right; they are desperate to be seen as righteous in the eyes of God. They seek first the kingdom of God and His righteousness. In the everyday pace of our world, we press hard to develop our skills and expertise, but the chosen develop their integrity and their hearts.

The chosen also carry what I call a mantle of humility. The Bible says that God resists the proud but gives grace to the humble (Jas. 4:6). The chosen know this and seek in all things to remain humble. In the world's eyes humility, brokenness, and submission are seen as weaknesses, but in the chosen realm they are the secret to spiritual strength and grace. For it is in our weakness that He is strong. (See 2 Corinthians 12:9.)

The heart of the chosen is heavy with the eternal weight of God's glory. They are a presence people. They love the glory of God and love to create an atmosphere where God's presence can dwell. This happens not only in worship but also in their everyday lives—coming and going and carrying out their divine assignments. Their entire lifestyle reflects their heart of worship and love for God. They sense the great responsibility God has placed on them to fill the earth with His glory.

The heart of the chosen is worship. When they need to hear from God, they worship. In times of perplexity they worship. When they worship, wisdom and wealth come. There are things God is trying to release that the chosen will have to worship to get—creativity, ideas, solutions, and more.

For some of you, having a heart after God is your one desire. However, you may find yourself in a place where you feel as if you have lost favor in the presence of the Lord—where you once experienced an open heaven, and now it feels as if something has shifted. First, I want you to know that there are seasons to the chosen life. We all go through spring, winter, summer, and fall in the spirit. I talk about these different seasons in my book *The Deborah Anointing*, so I won't go into detail here. But there are times like the winter season when God is dealing with our character and preparing to launch us to a new place.

Without the correction and discipline of the winter season, we cannot sustain the overflow of blessing and increase that comes in the next season.

But as you look with expectancy toward the next season on your chosen path, I want to give you some things God has given me that will help you sustain an open heaven. The desire of a chosen one is to always be in a place of favor with God. We desire with our whole being to be pleasing to God. When heaven is open over our lives, when God's face shines upon us, and when we are in open communication with Him, hearing His voice at every offer of prayer, praise, and petition, our hearts are centered in God. No feeling is more glorious. We know that sin and unrighteousness can take us out of that place, but there are also times when God is silent, which for the chosen has less to do with our falling out of favor and more to do with His preparing us for even more.

God is building momentum. His power and glory are on the rise. They are increasing day by day. So don't get caught up in what you see around you. Keep your eyes set on things above. Anything that is in the way of your heart being centered on your one affection is being removed. As we discussed in chapter 6, strongholds are being broken off the minds and family lines of the chosen. So while you may not be feeling as though you are at the center of God's heart, know that you are. For He chose you and appointed you to bear fruit. You dwell in the glory cloud. You are of a presence people. You will see great manifestations of the glory of God because all that you need is in His glory. Healing is in the glory. Deliverance is in the glory. Wealth is in the glory. Strategies are in the glory. God is releasing a fresh dimension of His glory to you because you are one after His own heart.

When God releases His power to us through gifts and the anointing, we have to keep the momentum going. It's not a time to relax; it's time to press in to God. It is time to keep our hearts stirred through worship, prayer, Bible study, and faith. It's a season when His grace is on our lives and we feel the wind of His Spirit against our back, propelling us forward. To keep our hearts primed with the energy of God's presence, we must learn how to move with God. This is where obedience comes in.

A HEART OF OBEDIENCE

As we enter into seasons when God is releasing great increase of His power and glory, we have to learn to capitalize on it. Obedience helps us maintain our position in God. As He told Esau in Genesis 4:7, "If you do right, will you not be accepted?" Obedience is the way that we demonstrate our heart of love for God. Jesus said, "If you love Me, keep My commandments" (John 14:15). There is no substitute for obedience. The psalmist David—the one who God said had His heart—said, "For You do not desire sacrifice, or else I would give it; You do not delight in burnt offering. The sacrifices of God are a broken spirit, a broken and a contrite heart—these, O God, You will not despise" (Ps. 51:16–17). The word *contrite* in this verse means "to be crushed."[1] *Merriam-Webster's* dictionary defines it as "feeling or showing sorrow and remorse for a sin or shortcoming," "apologetic," or "repentant."[2] God accepts the heart that obeys and the one that repents when we fall short.

Imagine for a moment that God is speaking certain assignments to your heart, and then He says, "I want you to go on a three-day fast." But you are just coming off a fast and say, "Oh, God, I just fasted for three days last month right after that conference I attended."

As the heart of a chosen one develops in you, you will come to know the importance of obeying God even when it seems difficult or unusual. Sure, you fasted then. Don't you think God knows that? Was He not with you at the time? What He may be steering you toward is a different or fresh impartation. He wants to prepare you to receive the fullness of a new understanding about something that will help you in the next season.

Two things are important to remember: 1) God is committed to your growth and success. 2) The chosen realm is about operating in both the natural and supernatural realms with ease and great skill. You cannot waver in your obedience to God. An obedient heart is a steadfast and stable heart. Double-mindedness will get you nowhere fast. Obedience breaks stagnancy and puts you back in position to hear from God again.

God wants His chosen ones to maintain a steadiness of heart so that He can download new things on the inside of you so you can fulfill your purpose.

A HEART OF DESTINY AND PURPOSE

God wants to create in every one of us a heart for purpose and destiny. He wants us to make decisions according to His purpose. He gives us the spirit of wisdom so that we know how to operate in our season. The Bible tells us that there's a time and a season for everything. Perhaps

God gave you an instruction to do something two months ago, and it didn't work. It could be that there is a season coming when you will be under an open heaven, and it will be easier for you, and it will work. Sometimes we hear a word from the Lord ahead of the season for which it is to be accomplished. We must tap into God's heart to hear when the season to act is upon us. When we are acting in season, the limitations in our lives are broken.

God is releasing new assignments to His chosen ones in this hour. We must have a heart after His to sense what it is He is commissioning us to do. We must have the mindset to carry it out. We must know who we are in Him and in the earth. We must know our measure of rule. Some of us will be great entrepreneurs building companies that rebuild the economies in our communities and neighborhoods, creating jobs and opportunities for growth. Others of us will plant and build churches. The destiny and purpose for the chosen are to build the kingdom of God in the geographic regions to which we've been sent and within the realm of our giftings.

We must be freed from lifelong cycles of dysfunction and things that have happened in our bloodlines. God is delivering His chosen ones so they can be free to be His appointed glory carriers. He is calling each of us to be the best in the bunch, the first in our families, if necessary. If no one else is striving for freedom and prosperity, goodness and the favor of God, we are the ones who will. We will be the anointed ones to break every generational dysfunction. We will be the ones He will use to break the spirits of poverty, lack, and ignorance. There is a fresh download of the wisdom of God and prosperity. There is a fresh download of angelic assistance and keys of authority.

He is releasing all the resources of heaven to set you on the path of destiny and purpose. Therefore, we have to posture our hearts in this season to walk circumspectly.

A HEART OF REPENTANCE

Repentance is how we get back on God's time clock and back in step with Him on the path of life. Repentance corrects our spiritual sight when we have missed God. When we understand that God is not moving in the same way He moved yesterday, we will see things differently. We will have a different perspective. Based on the new perspective, we will get a strong unction toward repentance.

Saying sorry for this or sorry for that is not true repentance. True repentance means that, based on new information or a new encounter with the Lord, you now have the impetus to turn from your old ways. Now that you see yourself in your sin or wrong thinking and in the light of God's glory, you turn. Now that you see your lack of commitment or whatever character issue He shows you in the light of God's glory, you turn. Now that you understand why heaven, the kingdom, church, and the times of gathering are so important, you turn. You turn around 180 degrees and go in the opposite direction of where you had been going before. That is repentance. You turn from your sin when you have seen it exposed to the light of God's truth.

A great turning of the hearts of God's people is coming. At the start of this chapter I discussed how to sustain an open heaven. Keeping an open heaven over your life has everything to do with the posture of your heart. The hearts of the chosen dwell under an open heaven because they keep their hearts right. This is not about perfection. We can confidently say, after reading the stories, that David was not perfect, yet God called him a man after His own heart. David kept his heart open and honest with God. He submitted to God's correction many times over and repented quickly after he did wrong. The heavens were open over David's life, and he saw victory after victory.

A HEART OF LOVE

When the heavens are open, God begins to deal with our hearts. We begin to see ourselves and our calling the way God sees us and our callings. We've gotten ourselves in a bad fix when it comes to how we see ourselves, and this affects our ability to function according to how God created us. There's this issue of self-hatred that the devil has released on our generation, where we begin to hate ourselves. We don't like the shape of our noses. We don't like how we look. Perhaps without intending to, we are saying that we don't like the way God made us. We don't like the family we are in. It's almost a trend and something we have come to find comical at times—quirky self-deprecation. But it is a slippery slope right into hating God. We are made in the image of God. We are reflections of His glory on the earth. If we hate ourselves, we are hating God. We need healing. We need a heart change. We need a new perspective. We need to repent.

The Bible says that we should not think of ourselves more highly than we ought (Rom. 12:3). Many times religion interprets this scripture as, "You're too proud. You should be humble." Of course we should be humble, but we are powerful in the Lord. We are fearfully and wonderfully made. We can be humble without being self-hating, self-deprecating, and self-destructive.

God wants you to know that He made no mistake when He began to form you in your mother's womb. You were purposefully knit and woven together. Then He gave you an intellect, desires, and passions that led you to take on certain assignments and tasks that bring glory and honor to His name. He has preappointed your times and the boundaries of your dwelling. He knows why He put you in South Africa, Mexico, India, or the United Kingdom. He knows why He assigned you to the neighborhood and church you attend. He has fashioned all of this to get you to a place of fruitfulness, multiplication, destiny, and purpose. You cannot sustain an open heaven for these areas of your life if you do not love yourself and see yourself the way God sees you.

In Matthew 22:39 Jesus says, "You shall love your neighbor as yourself." If Jesus loves you enough and values you enough to die for you, you should love what He loves and value what He values. Then, understand this: you can only love others to the extent that you love yourself. Love for God and love for people are the overarching drivers for fulfilling your purpose.

Know that God loves you, and His hand of favor is on you. You are important to Him, and you are important to His plans and purposes on the earth.

OPEN HEART, OPEN HEAVEN

Let me give you a quick definition of *open heaven*. An open heaven is a pronounced increase in a particular season of the supernatural invading the natural.[3] It's a season that

God sets aside for a church, an individual, and sometimes a region when the supernatural power begins to invade the natural. When the heavens are open, God comes down and listens to you. Your spiritual senses sharpen, and you can hear differently. Just as you have natural senses, you also have spiritual senses. Just as you can see in the natural, the Holy Spirit will anoint you to see in the spirit.

You may ask, "Why do we need to see in the spirit?"

Because we've been walking past our blessings and divine opportunities, and we did not know it.

Two examples in Scripture speak of an open heaven from which we can pull strategies to implement in our lives that will help us sustain an open heaven. The first one is in Genesis 28:12–14:

> Then he dreamed, and behold, a ladder was set up on the earth, and its top reached to heaven; and there the angels of God were ascending and descending on it.
>
> And behold, the LORD stood above it and said: "I am the LORD God of Abraham your father and the God of Isaac; the land on which you lie I will give to you and your descendants. Also your descendants shall be as the dust of the earth; you shall spread abroad to the west and the east, to the north and the south; and in you and in your seed all the families of the earth shall be blessed."

Here's the picture: There was a ladder. When the heavens opened in Jacob's dream, angels began to ascend and descend. There was much activity. I see it as angels going up with prayers and coming down with answers. For us now, there is a spiritual ladder. This is a season when the heavens are open, and prayer is the key to keeping them open.

We pray. We declare. Accessing heaven is not only about binding and loosing. It's about your prayers going up and answers coming down. We need strategic answers, revelation, strategy, and direction in this season. We need to see heaven manifested in every area on the earth. An open heart of prayer makes this happen.

King Solomon is our second example. His prayer for wisdom in 1 Kings 3:6–9 demonstrates the heart of a chosen one, open to God to teach, lead, and provide heavenly resources as He calls us to a new assignment. Solomon prayed.

> You have shown great mercy to Your servant David my father, because he walked before You in truth, in righteousness, and in uprightness of heart with You; You have continued this great kindness for him, and You have given him a son to sit on his throne, as it is this day. Now, O LORD my God, You have made Your servant king instead of my father David, but I am a little child; I do not know how to go out or come in. And Your servant is in the midst of Your people whom You have chosen, a great people, too numerous to be numbered or counted. Therefore give to Your servant an understanding heart to judge Your people, that I may discern between good and evil. For who is able to judge this great people of Yours?

In this chapter I've brought attention to the characteristics of a chosen heart, and one of the most powerful characteristics is humility. Solomon had been raised in the royal courts of Israel. He grew up with the best and was afforded many privileges. But in his prayer he emphasized inexperience, a lack of knowledge, and inadequacy in being a king over God's chosen people. He knew well that in himself he didn't have what it took to lead them. This is the epitome of the humble heart of the chosen. He didn't shrink back and say, "No, God. You must have the wrong one. I can't do this. No, thank You." Instead, he saw himself through sober eyes and realized that without God's help, he would not be successful in taking on such a significant role. God doesn't always choose the qualified; He qualifies the chosen.

In Solomon's case God was so pleased at the posture of Solomon's heart that He opened the windows of heaven over His season of rule over Israel. This is what God said to him:

> Because you have asked this thing, and have not asked long life for yourself, nor have asked riches for yourself, nor have asked the life of your enemies, but have asked for yourself understanding to discern justice, behold, I have done according to your words; see, I have given you a wise and understanding heart, so that there has not been anyone like you before you, nor shall any like you arise after you. And I have also given you what you have not asked: both riches and honor, so that there shall not be anyone like you among the kings all your days. So if you walk in My ways, to keep My statutes and My commandments, as your father David walked, then I will lengthen your days.
>
> —1 KINGS 3:11–14

Solomon didn't devise or manipulate his prayer to God. Out of his heart flowed a prayer that revealed his ultimate desire, which was to bring honor and pleasure to God by leading His people well. James 4:3 says that when we pray, we ask and do not receive because we ask amiss or we ask with the wrong intentions and expectations. We ask so that we can spend what we get in answer to our prayers on our own pleasures. As I have said before, there is so much stored up for the righteous, but it will not be released to selfish, self-seeking, man-pleasing, pleasure-seeking hearts.

Great wealth is coming to the people whose hearts are after God. They have a great and mighty work to do that needs the things of heaven to be released so that they can get things done. Prayer is the key to releasing God's wisdom and wealth to His chosen ones.

When the heavens are open, angels begin to ascend and descend, moving on our behalf and in response to our prayers. As we look back at our first example of an open heaven, we see that with Jacob, God increased, expanded, and blessed his family and all their future generations. He said, "Also your descendants shall be as the dust of the earth; you shall spread abroad to the west and the east, to the north and the south; and in you and in your seed all the families of the earth shall be blessed" (Gen. 28:14).

When the heavens are open, God begins to spread out and breaks limitation off of your life. He wants to bless His chosen ones so that all the families of the earth are blessed. He wants to expand your measure of rule because there is no limit to the expansion of His kingdom. Why? Because God is with you, He put His name on you, and through your prayers you have caused heaven to open over you. Now angels are ascending and descending, moving on your behalf, carrying out the actions and commands of your prayers.

YOU ARE UNSTOPPABLE

When the heavens are open, nothing can stop you from walking in your destiny and accomplishing the purpose for which God has sent you. God needs you to get this perspective in your heart. Once God has decreed it in the heavens, it will be done on the earth. You are the only one who can stop your destiny. He told Jacob that He would be with him and keep him in every place he went. "[I] will bring you back to this land; for I will not leave you until I have done what I have spoken to you" (Gen. 28:15). Everything God decrees will be done.

God wants to increase our faith in this season. We must have faith, not in our ability but in His. We cannot look at ourselves, what we have, and where we come from. We must keep looking unto Jesus, the author and the finisher of our faith. We have to understand that He is the One who got this party started. He chose you. You are His idea. You are always on His mind. Psalm 139:17–18 says, "How precious also are Your thoughts to me, O God! How great is the sum of them! If I should count them, they would be more in number than the sand."

Can you count the granules of the sand? No one can count the granules. God is getting ready to bless us so much that it will be like the sand. It will be something we've never seen before. It's going to be so much that people will take notice just as the Queen of Sheba took notice of the great blessings God commanded toward

Solomon's life. When people come and ask you how and why, point them right back to Jesus.

God is making His chosen ones a sign and a wonder to this generation. A sign is a marking. God is putting a mark of distinction on us. We are assigned. We will be the ones who point people to Jesus.

THE GATES OF HEAVEN ARE OPEN

> Then Jacob awoke from his sleep and said, "Surely the LORD is in this place, and I did not know it." And he was afraid and said, "How awesome is this place! This is none other than the house of God, and this is the gate of heaven!"
>
> —GENESIS 28:16–17

Your prayers open the gates of heaven. This coexisting spiritual realm was always active, but Jacob didn't experience it until God opened his eyes. As you seek God in worship, prayer, and Bible study, and as the Holy Spirit opens your eyes and ears to the prophetic realm, blessings, miracles, God encounters, and awakenings will be your norm. Your prayers invoke the presence of El Shaddai, almighty God, in your situation. This is the name God called Himself in Genesis 28:13, where God established His presence in Jacob's life.

The name almighty God indicates all might, all power, all strength, and all sufficiency. Whenever God reveals His name, He is also revealing His nature, character, and attributes. When He reveals Himself as the almighty God, it also means that all might, all power, and all sufficiency are in me and in you. All of heaven is backing us up.

If you have a dream in your heart, now is the time to

put the business plan together because heaven is unlocking the resources for it. If you want to get that house, God is saying now is the time to get it because heaven is unlocking resources. If you need a miracle, God wants to release heaven's resources. Many miracles, signs, and wonders are waiting to be released in this generation. He just wants a hungry people—those who know how to open up the heavens, those who know how to worship Him, and those who know how to bless Him.

God wants to use His glory to open our eyes, ears, and hearts. He wants to heighten our supernatural ability. He wants to heighten our sensitivity to the happenings of the heavens and of the spirit realm. You have been chosen to carry the glory of God. You have been chosen to make His name famous. You have been chosen to operate in the blessings and to move in power. You have been chosen to move in demonstration. Do you know who you are?

If you have responded to God's call and accepted His plan for your life, "you are a holy people to the LORD your God, and the LORD has chosen you to be a people for Himself, a special treasure above all the peoples who are on the face of the earth" (Deut. 14:2). To you He says, "I am releasing and fulfilling every promise I made to you."

God has put things in your heart, things that you dreamed of, and at the time, you may have felt as though they were too hard to do for whatever reason, and you put them down. Let me tell you that God is breathing new life into those dreams. He is performing every promise and will do for you what you cannot do for yourself. This is what it means to have El Shaddai living on the inside of you.

God loves you, and He's ready to bless you. Remember, He chose you, and as you respond to the call, all the benefits of the chosen are prepared for you. He just needs a heart of commitment. The enemy will try to distract us with problems and get us away from the dreams and destiny God placed in our hearts. But instead of allowing the enemy to cheat you out of obtaining the promise and fulfilling your purpose, lift up your eyes and look unto Jesus. He has sent His Spirit to be your help. The maker of heaven and earth is ready to release His glory in your life. He is ready to release His favor in your life. All we have to do is keep that portal open with open hearts of prayer, humility, and obedience.

Chapter 10

UNAPOLOGETICALLY CHOSEN

Arise, shine; for thy light is come, and the glory
of the LORD is risen upon thee. For, behold, the
darkness shall cover the earth, and gross darkness
the people: but the LORD shall arise upon
thee, and his glory shall be seen upon thee.
—ISAIAH 60:1–2, KJV

SHINE BRIGHT—YOU are a chosen one. From this day
forth, don't let anybody cause you to dim your light.
In Matthew 5:14–16 Jesus said, "You're here to be
light, bringing out the God-colors in the world. God is not
a secret to be kept. We're going public with this, as public
as a city on a hill. If I make you light-bearers, you don't
think I'm going to hide you under a bucket, do you? I'm
putting you on a light stand. Now that I've put you there
on a hilltop, on a light stand—shine!" (MSG).

Many things have tried to put your light out, but Paul
says:

> But you are a chosen generation, a royal priesthood,
> a holy nation, His own special people, that you may
> proclaim the praises of Him who called you out of
> darkness into His marvelous light; who once were
> not a people but are now the people of God, who
> had not obtained mercy but now have obtained
> mercy.
>
> —1 PETER 2:9–10

Imagine now that the spotlight is on you. What are you going to do? You've been crying for open doors. You've been longing to see God do certain things in your family, church, community, and even the world. This book has opened up to you the wisdom, revelation, strategies, and plans that God has stored up for you to see the power of God manifested in each of these areas. We discussed what it takes to unlock them and begin to see them released in your own life.

We discussed the weight of glory attached to being a chosen one, and this is what I believe led you to pick up this book. You've known you were called. You've received the prophetic word, and perhaps you even had an encounter with God Himself. You can't ignore the voice of destiny calling out to you any longer. You know you were made for more, and you have decided that it is time. You are ready to accept the invitation and step into your role as a chosen one. Now the light of God is shining on you. What are you going to do with this new stage?

I'd like to challenge you to enter it with confidence. Walk right on to center stage. You were made for this moment. Arise. Stand in your place. Take the mic. Sing the song. Preach the sermon. Write the book. Start the business. Launch the ministry. It is showtime. It is time for you to be who God called you to be. The stage has been set, and the way has been prepared. Many have received the call. Many have the chance to affirm who they've been called to be. But only a few will do it, and you are one of the few. And you know what this means to me? You don't have to apologize for the stage you are on. You don't have to apologize for your gifts that are making room for you, sitting you before great men and women. You don't have to apologize for being sought out for the anointing on your life. Your light has come.

God knows this is a new level for you, but you have to take the risk. You will be doing Him a great disservice if you cower, sit back on your seat, and whine or deny the greatness that He has built inside you. He has opened up all of heaven to help you display His power and glory on the earth. Don't use the excuse that you don't have anyone to go with you to this next level. You can't wait for somebody to share your pulse and hold up what God is trying to do. You must arise.

Esther didn't know if she would have someone in the palace to help or protect her—and her calling and chosen season were initiated against her will—but God had a plan to circumvent the actions of evil men. Remember, plans change; purpose doesn't. God placed two people in key positions to help Esther assume her chosen role—the eunuch in charge of the king's harem and her uncle Mordecai, who served as an officer in the king's court. Both had positions of influence that helped Esther arise in her purpose. God has people waiting for you as well, but if you wait where you are because no one is validating you in your current position, you will miss out on seeing God positioning the people who will help you carry out your purpose.

Isaiah 60:1–2 says, "And the glory of the LORD is risen upon you. For behold, the darkness shall cover the earth, and deep darkness the people." So even as God is putting people in position to help you carry out your purpose, He is also rising upon you to strengthen and empower you to bring your light to dark places in the earth where people are dwelling in that deep darkness. When you hear about the increase in the numbers of people who are committing suicide, when you hear about tsunamis and earthquakes, or other political, social, economic, or natural disasters, you are hearing the groans of creation Paul spoke about in Romans 8. That is the darkness that is upon the earth. You may start looking around and wondering, "Who is going to do something about this? Somebody ought to do something. Somebody ought to say something." That person is you, beloved.

You and God are the majority—you and God and your angels of destiny.

> But the LORD will arise over you, and His glory will
> be seen upon you. The Gentiles shall come to your
> light, and kings to the brightness of your rising.
> —ISAIAH 60:2–3

You don't need any more permission to carry the glory. God is arising over you, activating you into your destiny. No longer are you a lightweight; you carry a weight of glory, one of honor, splendor, and power. These are days of unusual breakthrough for the chosen. God is awakening you to your passion. You don't need to apologize for what

God is doing in your life—for blessing, favor, and being chosen. I want to leave you with some strategies that will help you see God fully break you through from where you are into something new. They are found in 2 Chronicles 20.

SEEK THE LORD AND PROCLAIM A FAST

Coming back to this passage from our discussion of it in chapter 8, we are going to look at it from another perspective. We had seen it before in terms of the angelic support God released from heaven on the Israelites' behalf. What I want to show you here is how they ended up in a three-day collection of spoils from this battle because there was just so much bounty. I also want to show you how this reflects the transfer of wealth and resources the chosen will experience as we get in position and follow the strategies God lays out for us when we seek Him. This is where we start in this passage, 2 Chronicles 20:3–5:

> And Jehoshaphat feared, and set himself to seek the LORD, and proclaimed a fast throughout all Judah. So Judah gathered together to ask help from the LORD; and from all the cities of Judah they came to seek the LORD. Then Jehoshaphat stood in the assembly of Judah and Jerusalem, in the house of the LORD, before the new court.

Once we have accepted the call and taken up our chosen life, there will be a different kind of enemy formed against us. Jehoshaphat was the new king and had come into his position with a heart after God. He had made some reforms to restore righteous judges throughout the land, reinstate the Levitical priesthood in the temple, and end the worship of idols. Israel had been under the rule of wicked and idolatrous kings, and he came in and reversed all the evil they had done in the eyes of the Lord. (You can see this part of the story in 2 Chronicles 19.)

Jehoshaphat was a chosen one, and upon stepping up to do what he had been placed there to do, he received word in 2 Chronicles 20:2 that a "great multitude" was coming against him and his people. We too must understand that a "great multitude" will be formed against us as we arise in our chosen destiny. The enemy will not let this happen without great resistance. However, we must repent and be willing to tear down the beliefs and mindsets that would prevent us from taking our worthy walk as the chosen. We discussed what some of these are in an earlier chapter. We must be walking in the spirit to understand what's happening, to begin to discern the time, and to call ourselves to times of fasting and prayer in order to seek the Lord. No matter how big the problem is—how great the multitude is—it's not bigger than God. I have spent my life in the last two months defending the integrity and the bigness of God. Let's look at verse 6:

> Jehoshaphat...said: "O LORD, God of our fathers, are You not God in heaven, and do You not rule over all the kingdoms of the nations, and in Your hand is there not power and might, so that no one is able to withstand You?"

You have to remind yourself who God is. You cannot afford to waffle in unbelief. Your study and knowledge of the character and attributes of God will strengthen your faith. You will begin to remind God of who you know

Him to be and what you know His promises are for you. Isaiah 62:6 says, "You who [are His servants and by your prayers] put the Lord in remembrance [of His promises], keep not silence" (AMPC).

This is what Jehoshaphat began to do. He reminded God of who he knew Him to be, and he made these declarations in front of the people. These are days to proclaim the name of the Lord and begin to magnify Him above the enemies you may face as you enter this new realm. Praise is the expression of a voice of faith. When you begin to praise God, your heart and mind are set in faith, which then overflows into your mouth and aligns to show you who God is and what you believe about what He will do to break you through. When you can't praise God, it's because you don't know who He is and you don't have the faith you need to stand in place and see His salvation from the hand of this great multitude forming against you.

The gift of faith is being released in this hour, and God will call the high praises to be in your mouth and the two-edged sword in your hand to execute His plans. But to gain victory over that multitude, you must first open your mouth and let declarations of who God is arise so that He will be reminded—so that you will be reminded—that the victory is already yours. The devil will try to muscle you with fear, failure, shame, and defeat. This is why you need to call yourself to a season of fasting and centering your mind on the Lord to hear Him, to increase your level of faith, and while you are reminding Him, your heart is being strengthened to carry out the strategies He releases.

WORSHIP

Then look what happened. Second Chronicles 20:13–14 (KJV) says, "And all Judah stood before the LORD, with their little ones, their wives, and their children. Then upon Jahaziel the son of Zechariah, the son of Benaiah, the son of Jeiel, the son of Mattaniah, a Levite of the sons of Asaph, came the Spirit of the LORD in the midst of the congregation," and he began to prophesy.

We see in this verse where it says "with their little ones." Being chosen and expanding into new territories— expanding the kingdom—is about the generations and legacy. The chosen are a presence generation. The presence of God accompanies worship. When we worship and magnify God above the approaching enemy, we are not just doing this for the battle today. We are doing this to extend the voice of faith through praise even to our children and their children and beyond that. What we do today as we arise as chosen ones is not just about us today; it's about legacy. The enemy is after our children. He's after our legacy. This is all the more reason that you must stand up and lift your voice unto God. Don't let the enemy keep you quiet.

The people of Israel were in a place where they could do nothing in their own strength. They were in a spiritual battle much like we are today. We are in a battle of belief at its most basic level. We arm ourselves with the faith of God and His Word, and the enemy sends a great multitude of things to tear down that faith. He starts with planting thoughts, ideas, and arguments that rise up against what we know of God and what He has spoken to us: "You're too old for this." "You should have started this a long time ago." "It's too late now." Shut him down with your voice of faith. Your praise, magnification of God, and your actions arise and communicate your refusal to let his attempts stop you. In essence, you will be fighting back and saying, "It is my time. I do have more destiny in me. You may be trying to convince me that there's nothing for me, but there must be something for me because if there was nothing, you wouldn't be saying anything." The great multitude would not have formed if the people of Israel had posed no threat. Remember that.

REST IN THE LORD

> And he said, "Listen, all you of Judah and you inhabitants of Jerusalem, and you, King Jehoshaphat! Thus says the LORD to you: 'Do not be afraid nor dismayed because of this great multitude, for the battle is not yours, but God's.'"
> —2 CHRONICLES 20:15

There are some things you will not have to fight. I know you may be saying, "But I'm a warrior. I bind, and I loose. I sling my anointing oil." I am the same way, but the Lord had to calm me down. He said, "I don't want you to do that this time."

Sometimes nothing is the hardest thing to do for people like us who are full of resources, ways, and intelligence. Perhaps you are like me and have been serving the Lord for more than twenty-five years. Or maybe you were born into a family of believers and came to faith at a young age. All you've known is how to put up a defense against the enemy. You've been trained in deliverance, been activated in prophetic ministry, served in apostolic functions, and put together programs and revivals. But instead of doing more, God says rest.

Then the Bible says, "'You will not need to fight in this battle. Position yourselves, stand still and see the salvation of the LORD, who is with you, O Judah and Jerusalem!' Do not fear or be dismayed; tomorrow go out against them, for the LORD is with you" (2 Chron. 20:17).

Sometimes you have to shut your mouth and not say another word. Just pull back. Position yourself in a posture of surrender. Stand still in the presence of God. Surrender all of your efforts and methods of fighting in your own power, and give it all to God. You may not know how the battle will be won. We discussed how it is not always necessary to know all the details if you trust and know God. Start with the one thing God has told you. You may not know where the money is going to come from, but what you do know is that the Lord is good and His mercy endures forever. You know that many are they that set themselves against you, but the Lord is your shield, your glory, and lifter up of your head. You know God prevails.

We cannot be like what I call "power Christians," who go to church every week but won't believe God. They trust in the armor of flesh. They trust in the armor of their jobs. They trust in somebody promoting them, but they won't trust God. "Some trust in chariots and horses," the Bible says, "but I will trust in the name of the Lord." Chariots and horses represent the systems of man. We cannot put our trust in those things and think we will get the victory.

The devil keeps trying to get us to walk in the flesh. He tries to catch us up into arguments. Anytime you get into that doubt, you are dabbling with what the Bible calls "an evil heart of unbelief" (Heb. 3:12). But when we trust God, all arguments are silenced and we can enter into a place of surrender.

BELIEVE GOD

> So they rose early in the morning and went out into the Wilderness of Tekoa; and as they went out, Jehoshaphat stood and said, "Hear me, O Judah and you inhabitants of Jerusalem: Believe in the LORD your God, and you shall be established; believe His prophets, and you shall prosper."
> —2 CHRONICLES 20:20

As I've already mentioned, as you enter the chosen realm, the devil will try to attack your faith. You are advancing into a place of destiny and purpose. Your occupation of enemy territory is expanding. Now more than ever, you need to believe God. No matter how insurmountable the situation looks, believe God. The prophet in the previous verse was saying, "Believe me. Hear me." I encourage you to hear God. "Faith comes by hearing, and hearing by the word of God" (Rom. 10:17).

I rebuke all dullness of hearing. I pray for a fresh spirit of revelation to come upon your life, that you will have ears to hear what the Spirit is saying to you and about your destiny. You will hear clearly. I command those voices that come against your life—voices of failure and defeat—to be silent in the name of Jesus, that you will hear the word of the Lord for your life.

Believe in the Lord your God, and you shall be established. Believe in His prophets, and you will prosper in the chosen place.

RELEASE THE VOICE OF FAITH

> And when he had consulted with the people, he
> appointed those who should sing to the LORD, and
> who should praise the beauty of holiness, as they
> went out before the army and were saying: "Praise
> the LORD, for His mercy endures forever."
>
> —2 CHRONICLES 20:21

God said, "Tell my people praise is the voice of faith." I
touched on this just previously that when you believe,
you have a corresponding action of praise because of
who God is. So if you are not praising, that means you
don't have faith in God. What God knows, which you
may sometimes lose sight of in the midst of the threat of
battle, is that praise will also bind and confuse the enemy.
Second Chronicles 20:22 says, "Now when they began to
sing and to praise, the LORD set ambushes against the
people of Ammon, Moab, and Mount Seir, who had come
against Judah; and they were defeated."

These instructions to sing and praise are not deep
Hebrew and Greek. Religion always wants to make victory
hard to come by—and in some cases it is, but again, you
will not fight every battle and every enemy the same way.
This is the way that God led the people under Jehoshaphat,
the one who had a heart after God, who had been chosen,
who reestablished a holy and righteous order in the
kingdom and in the temple. He did not have to fight this
battle the way other kings fought. I want to challenge you
to see how God will lead you to fight, as you too are a
chosen one, with a heart after God, one who has been sent
to establish the glory and holiness and majesty of God in
the sphere of the earth God has set you over.

We feel as if we always have to perform, but we don't—not when God is fighting the battle. The people sang and praised the Lord while God destroyed every one of their enemies. No one escaped. When God destroys your enemy, it is finished. You will not have to keep looking over your shoulder. He will clear the path for you to advance into the territory He's called you to.

COLLECT THE SPOILS

> When Jehoshaphat and his people came to take away their spoil, they found among them an abundance of valuables on the dead bodies, and precious jewelry, which they stripped off for themselves, more than they could carry away; and they were three days gathering the spoil because there was so much.
> —2 CHRONICLES 20:25

The chosen need resources and wealth to carry out the assignments God is delegating. The Bible talks about a transference of wealth from the wicked to the just, and I believe we are heading into a time when there will be the greatest transfer of wealth we have ever seen. No longer will the wealth just be laid up, but God is going to transfer the wealth to you. But it will take some unconventional actions to gather it all. The people of Israel had to pull stuff off of dead bodies. Whatever the dead bodies represent along your chosen journey, God will reveal, and you will do just as He commands if you want to recover the spoils. You can be religious sitting in the church if you want to, praising God with your tambourine, but if you want the wealth that is laid up for you, you will need to follow God's instruction and go where He sends you to get your stuff. He has already slayed your enemies. They are lying at your feet. You now have to do the work and gather the riches and wealth that will fund your chosen assignment.

I know what that means for me. God has shown me that I have houses and cities to build. There are people He wants me to send to school. This is not a small man's mentality. The work God is calling us to do will require spoils that take three days to gather.

I decree right now that you will see your life differently, that you will get out of that small-man's thinking, that you will see the great paradigm- and economy-shifting things God is calling you to do, that you will come to understand the need for the great transfer of wealth that's coming, and you will put a demand on its arrival. This transfer will be unusual and unprecedented. You will not be able to explain it. To be in a mindset to take advantage of what God is about to do, you must get delivered from the fear of the opinions of men. Your concern with what he says, what they say, how she does that, and why they are doing it will hinder you from following God into this place that those with carnal minds will not understand.

You must get delivered from that because if God is going to do these things in your life that you can't even explain, you don't want to miss it. All you should want is to be in the mindset to say, "The Lord is good, and His mercy endures forever." Again, this is about the excellency of God, not of us.

GET LOW

Remember, He said in 2 Chronicles 20:17 to position yourself. God wants us to change our position from always fighting in the flesh. Instead, He wants us to get low, get on our knees because He wants to bless us. Verse 26 says:

> And on the fourth day they assembled in the Valley of Berachah, for there they blessed the LORD; therefore the name of that place was called The Valley of Berachah until this day.

The physical location of Berachah has a spiritual meaning that I couldn't get past. The Lord kept highlighting it. When I looked it up, I saw that it meant kneeling in relation to being in position to receive a blessing or benediction. It also meant blessing, prosperity, a gift, or present.[1] Then God said to me, "Tell My people that as they continue to kneel, I will endue them with power for success."

Berachah is a place of prosperity and longevity for success. It is a place God will lead you to on your chosen journey to give you what you need for the work ahead—to be fruitful and multiply, to subdue and take dominion. He is leading you to this place, Berachah, where you will be endued with power for longevity and success, with power to prosper and get wealth. You are heading into a valley of blessing. This is our birthright, our inheritance with the saints. We do not need to apologize for what God has made available to all but to which only few have accepted.

The chosen life is not easy because of what God requires and what our flesh rebels against—holiness, righteousness, humility, being set apart, refinement by fire, the chastening of the Lord. But it also comes with blessings and

favor untold, intimacy with God, a place in the heavenlies to administrate the kingdom, having direct influence
in both heaven and the earth realms. There is no life like
the chosen life because there is no one like the God of the
chosen.

One of the most important parts of being a chosen one
is staying in the right posture of heart that allows you con-
tinual access to the Spirit of God. We must walk by the
Spirit to hear what the Spirit is saying and to do what He
is saying we should do. There is so much depending on
our ability to hear so that we are in the right place at the
right time, doing the right thing with the right people. We
need to hear so that we do not miss out on the opportunities to shine bright the light of God in the dark places in
the earth and be mighty vessels through which His power
and glory are made known among the children of men.

> But you are a chosen generation, a royal priesthood,
> a holy nation, His own special people, that you may
> proclaim the praises of Him who called you out of
> darkness into His marvelous light.
>
> —1 PETER 2:9

Arise and step into the marvelous light of God. Your
chosen life awaits.

NOTES

CHAPTER 1
THE CHOSEN REALM

1.   Blue Letter Bible, s.v. "*nĕshamah*," accessed June 13, 2019, https://www.blueletterbible.org/lang/lexicon/lexicon .cfm?Strongs=H5397&t=KJV.

2.   Blue Letter Bible, s.v. "*nĕshamah*."

3.   "William Seymour and the History of the Azusa Street Outpouring," The Revival Library, accessed June 13, 2019, http:// www.revival-library.org/index.php/pensketches-menu/american -pentecostal-pioneers/william-seymour.

4.   Blue Letter Bible, s.v. "*charis*," accessed June 13, 2019, https://www.blueletterbible.org/lang/lexicon/lexicon .cfm?Strongs=G5485&t=KJV.

5.   Blue Letter Bible, s.v. "*charisma*," accessed June 13, 2019, https://www.blueletterbible.org/lang/lexicon/lexicon .cfm?Strongs=G5486&t=KJV.

6.   *Merriam-Webster*, s.v. "wit," accessed June 13, 2019, https://www.merriam-webster.com/dictionary/wit.

7.   *Merriam-Webster*, s.v. "wit."

8.   *Merriam-Webster*, s.v. "wit."

CHAPTER 2
THE PATH OF THE CHOSEN

1.   Blue Letter Bible, s.v. "*luwz*," accessed June 13, 2019, https://www.blueletterbible.org/lang/lexicon/lexicon .cfm?Strongs=H3868&t=KJV.

2.   *Merriam-Webster*, s.v. "perverse," accessed June 13, 2019, https://www.merriam-webster.com/dictionary/perverse.

3.   *Oxford Living Dictionaries*, s.v. "*expectation*," accessed June 13, 2019, https://en.oxforddictionaries.com /definition/expectation.

CHAPTER 3
CHOSEN TIMES AND APPOINTMENTS

1.   Blue Letter Bible, s.v. *"chronos,"* accessed June 13, 2019, https://www.blueletterbible.org/lang/lexicon/lexicon .cfm?strongs=G5550.

2.   Blue Letter Bible, s.v. *"kairos,"* accessed June 13, 2019, https://www.blueletterbible.org/lang/lexicon/lexicon .cfm?strongs=G2540.

CHAPTER 4
CHOSEN TO WALK BY THE SPIRIT

1.   Blue Letter Bible, s.v. *"phroneō,"* accessed June 13, 2019, https://www.blueletterbible.org/lang/lexicon/lexicon .cfm?Strongs=G5426&t=KJV.

2.   Blue Letter Bible, s.v. *"endyō,"* accessed June 13, 2019, https://www.blueletterbible.org/lang/lexicon/lexicon .cfm?Strongs=G1746&t=KJV.

3.   Blue Letter Bible, s.v. *"nasag,"* accessed June 13, 2019, https://www.blueletterbible.org/lang/lexicon/lexicon .cfm?Strongs=H5381&t=KJV.

CHAPTER 5
SOZO: UNLOCKING THE FULLNESS OF GOD'S PLAN FOR YOUR LIFE

1.   Blue Letter Bible.org, s.v. *"sōtēria,"* accessed June 14, 2019, https://www.blueletterbible.org/lang/lexicon/lexicon .cfm?Strongs=G4991&t=KJV.

2.   Bible Study Tools, s.v. *"sozo,"* accessed June 13, 2019, https://www.bibletools.org/index.cfm/fuseaction/Lexicon.show /ID/G4982/sozo.htm.

CHAPTER 6
UNGODLY BELIEFS AND MINDSETS THAT ATTACK THE CHOSEN

1.   Leland Ryken, *Words of Delight: A Literary Introduction to the Bible* (Grand Rapids, MI: Baker Books, 1993), https://books .google.com/books?id=S24fAc1UFLwC&q.

2.   Yaacov Cohen, "The Tragic Life of Queen Esther," HuffPost, April 22, 2013, https://www.huffpost.com/entry/the -tragic-life-of-queen-esther_b_2722130.

CHAPTER 7
THE CHOSEN ARE FILLED WITH THE KNOWLEDGE OF GOD'S WILL

1.   *Merriam-Webster,* s.v. "full," accessed June 13, 2019, https://www.merriam-webster.com/dictionary/full.

2.   Goalcast.com, "C. S. Lewis Quote," accessed June 13, 2019, https://www.goalcast.com/2018/03/26/15-c-s-lewis-quotes /c-s-lewis-quote1/.

3.   Blue Letter Bible, s.v. "*klēsis,*" accessed June 13, 2019, https://www.blueletterbible.org/lang/lexicon/lexicon .cfm?Strongs=G2821&t=KJV.

CHAPTER 8
ANGELS ASSIGNED TO YOUR DESTINY

1.   Blue Letter Bible, s.v. "*Machanayim,*" accessed July 11, 2019, https://www.blueletterbible.org/lang/Lexicon/Lexicon. cfm?strongs=H4266&t=KJV.

2.   Blue Letter Bible, s.v. "*nataph,*" accessed July 11, 2019, https://www.blueletterbible.org/lang/Lexicon/Lexicon. cfm?strongs=H5197&t=KJV.

3.   Blue Letter Bible, s.v. "*marar,*" accessed July 11, 2019, https://www.blueletterbible.org/lang/Lexicon/Lexicon. cfm?strongs=H4843&t=KJV.

CHAPTER 9
THE HEART OF THE CHOSEN

1.   Blue Letter Bible, s.v. "*dakah,*" accessed June 13, 2019, https://www.blueletterbible.org/lang/lexicon/lexicon .cfm?Strongs=H1794&t=KJV.

2.   *Merriam-Webster,* s.v. "contrite," accessed June 13, 2019, https://www.merriam-webster.com/dictionary/contrite#synonyms.

3.   Definition derived from Chihop.org, accessed June 13, 2019, https://chihop.org/resources/glossary-of-terms/.

CHAPTER 10
UNAPOLOGETICALLY CHOSEN

1.   Blue Letter Bible, s.v. *"Bĕrakah,"* accessed June 13, 2019, https://www.blueletterbible.org/lang/lexicon /lexicon.cfm?Strongs=H1294&t=KJV; s.v. *"Bĕrakah,"* https://www .blueletterbible.org/lang/lexicon/lexicon .cfm?strongs=H1293&t=KJV.

MY **FREE** GIFTS TO YOU

Thank You

FOR READING *CHOSEN*

MANY ARE CALLED, BUT YOU ARE CHOSEN.
I am so happy you read my book. I hope you
have been equipped with prophetic insight
and divine strategies that will jump-start
you on the path toward destiny.

**AS MY WAY OF SAYING
THANK YOU... I AM OFFERING
YOU A COUPLE OF GIFTS:**

- E-book: *The Hannah Anointing*
- E-book: *The Deborah Anointing*
- E-book: *Prayers and Declarations
  for the Woman of God*

To get these FREE GIFTS, please go to:
www.MichelleMcClainBooks.com/gift

Thanks again and God bless you,

Michelle McClain-Walters